Landmark Visitor

Lesv

Brian & Eileen Anderson

Published by
Landmark Publishing
Ashbourne Hall, Cokayne Ave, Ashbourne,
Derbyshire DE6 1EJ England

Opposite: Molyvos harbour with the castle in the background

Landmark Visitors Guide

Lesvos

Brian & Eileen Anderson

Contents

Contents

Maps

1 Introduction

If you are tired of overdeveloped high rise and crowded holiday resorts, then Lesvos could be the perfect antidote. Physically and culturally, it has barely changed over recent years. We lived there in 1985/6 and fell in love with the island then and have been regular visitors ever since. Somehow it missed out on the first tourism boom to hit Greece. The infrastructure was not ready. For an island as large as Lesvos, something like three times the size of Corfu, and so under populated, it took some time to get modern road systems in place. By the time is was ready, the island was in a position to look how tourism had developed throughout the Mediterranean. It decided to be different and promote its very best features, a peaceful and beautiful countryside, traditional villages, bountiful olive groves and abundant, unspoilt natural history.

It is like turning the clock back to find a Greek island of yesteryear. There are villages tucked away in the mountains where seeing a tourist is an event, where men spend their mornings adorning taverna tables in the narrow streets, idly fingering komboloi beads and arguing politics; villages where you will be greeted warmly but where a taverna owner might just be a little nervous at understanding your requirements. This refreshing slow pace of life is the essence of holidays on this island.

When you are ready to tear yourself away from the beaches, and there are some good beaches on Lesvos (see Good Beach Guide), there is plenty of sightseeing ranging right across the island. There are castles, gulfs, Turkish minarets and little explored ancient sites where you might have to do your own interpretation. Better still, there are footpaths and old donkey trails leading through the mountainous countryside offering walking of all grades as good and as spectacular as any found anywhere in the Mediterranean (see Walking in the Factfile). Be sure to take binoculars too for Lesvos is one of the best birding sites in Europe, and a good flower book too for the spring display of wild orchids and flowers in general.

So a little known Greek island awaits your pleasure. Timeless as it might seem, enjoy it now before it changes.

LOCATION

Lesvos is tucked away in the north east Aegean on the edge of Europe, a mere five nautical miles from Turkey, close enough to see easily from the north and west coasts. It is a large island, the third largest in Greece after Evia and Crete, with a land area of 629.5 square miles

(1,630sq km). Unusually for an island, it is almost triangular in shape, and is penetrated by two deep gulfs each with a narrow mouth. Both gulfs exit to the sea on the south of the island with the Gulf of Gera on the western side and the Gulf of Kalloni more central. The Gulf of Kalloni is the longer with a length of 12.5 miles (20km) compared to the Gulf of Yera at 7.5 miles (12km).

Both gulfs once teemed with fish, especially sardines and shellfish, which in the past graced the banquet tables of Rome. In more recent times, tanneries along the Gulf of Gera used to pollute the fishing there and this is recovering but the Gulf of Kalloni is clean and remains well known for its sardines.

Mountains dominate the island, although none of them have any great height. Olympos, near Agiassos, which is a much smaller cousin of the home of the gods on the mainland, and Lepetimnos in the north both rise to a height of about 3,175 ft (968m). There are few plains with the one at the head of the Gulf of Kalloni easily the largest.

Volcanic activity stretching back over 20 million years, which created the petrified forest, effectively swamped the existing geology in the western part of the island and major volcanic craters have been identified in central Lesvos. The volcanic landscape is most clearly evident in the extreme west where the hillsides are barren and only the valley bottoms are green. Travelling west to east, the change in the landscapes is dramatic. As the hard, unyielding volcanic rocks are left behind, the vegetation increases steadily until the limestone regions of the east are reached where the vegetation is rich and abundant. Lesvos is virtually two islands in one. A harsh, barren west and a green, lush east. Olives are grown as a virtual monoculture, there are eleven million trees on the island and most of those grow to the east of Kalloni.

The unstable subterranean structure, indicated by past earthquake activity, is also responsible for the numerous hot springs which occur around the island.

Lesbos, Lesvos or Mytilene?

Understandably, there is some confusion amongst visitors regarding the modern name of the island. Although the written name is Lesbos, the pronunciation is Lesvos. Locals actually use Mytilene, after the main town, which was the official name of the island for a time in the Middle Ages. If you are travelling internally within Greece, by air or by ferry, departure boards will show only times to Mytilene with no reference at all to Lesvos.

Internationally, the island remains known as Lesvos and the islanders prefer that it is both written and pronounced as Lesvos which makes the inhabitants Lesvians.

WHEN TO GO

April is about the earliest that can be considered for a holiday, although birders and walkers may choose to go earlier. Even in April there is a risk that the weather may be cold and showery but, if the sun is shining, the island is at its most beautiful. At this time the sea is still cold but the sun is easily hot enough to burn and sunbathers still need to take care. Spring is a delightful season for colour when the trees are vivid green and the wild flowers at their very best. Fortunately, the spring flowers extend into May and May is generally more reliable for weather. Daytime temperatures start to rise but the evenings are still cool. It is not always warm enough to dine outside in the evening in the early part of the month but night-time temperatures too are on the rise and it soon becomes possible, well before the month is out.

Things warm up in June in every sense. The days and nights get hotter and the island tourist machine moves into top gear. Nowhere is too crowded and independent visitors can still expect to find accommodation without too much trouble. All that changes in July and August when the island is at its hottest and busiest.

Even the locals welcome September when the crowds start to depart and some of the intense heat leaves the sun. Many regard September as the best month of the summer with the sea still warm and the sun still pouring incessantly although there is the risk of an occasional thunderstorm. October is cooler with the possibility of more cloudy and rainy days but still with fine, sunny periods.

Activity Holidays

Visitors who go out into the countryside and enjoy the beauty of the island, through walking, bird watching, painting or enjoying the wild orchids and flowers are highly valued and actively encouraged. Not only does this help to extend the season but it helps to spread a little of the wealth away from the resorts into the countryside and helps to keep some of the smaller villages alive. April, the height of spring, is already turning into a busy month on Lesvos but there are plenty of alternative times for enjoying the natural beauty of this island.

Walkers: March, April, May, September and October are the best months, although February and November can provide good weather.

Wild Flower Enthusiasts: March, April and May are the best months for the spring display of wild flowers, although October can be good too for autumn flowers, especially cyclamen.

Bird Spotters: April and May are the best months to catch sight of the thousands of spring migrants which pass through and autumn to a lesser extent.

Painting: this is an anytime pursuit and there are plenty of scenic cameos all around the island to bring the sketch pad into operation or set up an easel

Landmark Hotspots

1 The Petrified Forest
A unique opportunity to look back at the species of trees foresting Lesvos 20 million years ago, now set in stone!

2 The spectacular mountain village of Agiassos
Set on the wooded slopes of mount Olympos, the winding, wisteria-decked streets of Agiassos ooze atmosphere and history. It also has one of the most important churches on the island.

3 Top tourist resort of Molyvos
Superb location on the north shore overlooked by an imposing castle. Narrow streets packed with shops leading up to the castle and an atmospheric harbour with good tavernas.

4 Mytilene, the capital city
Busy main town but with the best shopping on the island, a castle to see and two excellent archaeological museums.

5 The fishing village of Skala Sikaminias
A small but enchanting harbour on the north coast where there is nothing to do but drink in the sights and eat fish in the surrounding tavernas.

6 Ancient Aqueduct at Moria
Built in Roman times to carry water from Mount Olympos to Mytilene town, there is a large section still standing.

7 Limonas monastery
Well located in the centre of the island, just west of Kalloni, Limonas is one of the largest and most important monasteries on the island.

8 Atmospheric Petra
An old village, now a small resort, built around a huge rock towering vertically from the plain. A church sits on top of the rock.

9 Salt Pans
A visit to the salt pans, either near Kalloni or Skala Polichnitou, to see the flamingos and a host of other wading birds resident there.

10 Hot springs
Hot springs are one of the natural wonders on the island. There are a number to see but the best ones are at Gera, Lisvori or Polichnitos.

Below left: Patterns made where the hot spring emerge at Polichnitos
Below right: Vareltzidaina House museum in Petra

Molyvos harbour

WHERE TO STAY

There is not an abundance of resorts on the island and the following list is virtually comprehensive. The list starts from the capital and works around the island clockwise.

Mytilene Town: this is the busy capital of the island where almost one third of the island's population lives. It has no resort character although it does have a small town beach. There are numerous hotels near the water front which are handy for people arriving or departing with the ferry service. The best and most upmarket hotels lie just south of the town, between the town and the airport.

Ag Isidoros/Plomari: although these two lie on the south coast about 1.5 miles (2.4km) apart, they are usually linked together. Ag. Isidoros is the actual resort claiming a fine sandy beach and good accommodation while Plomari is a harbour town with some industry. It is famed around the island for its production of Plomari ouzo.

Vatera: lying on the south coast close to the entrance of the Gulf of Kalloni, Vatera is blessed with 5 miles (8km) of good beach. The resort has a small centre but it mainly straggles out along the beach. Plenty of hotels, bars and facilities but it remains a fairly quiet resort outside July and August. This one is destined to grow.

Skala Kallonis: located at the head of the Gulf of Kalloni, Skala Kallonis occupies pole position in a sense by being very centrally located on the island. It has a good village atmosphere with a small fishing port and a resident pelican! The beach too is good bordering the shallow waters of the gulf. With only five main hotels supported by village rooms, it does get full in April and early May with birders.

Skala

The names of many seaside villages on Lesvos start with the word Skala, Skala Eressou, Skala Kallonis, Skala Sikaminias, the list is quite long.

The word *skala* translates to steps, ladder or a landing stage and it is the latter meaning which is intended here. It originates from the days when the population settled inland away from the coast for security reasons. Even then it was important for the fishermen to be able to have somewhere safe to dock their boats so they built a '*skala*' on the nearest suitable stretch of coast. Eventually, as threats from the sea diminished, fishermen started to resettle their families around their boats so new villages started to grow and take the name of their original village prefixed by Skala. Almost every ancient settlement close to the sea has a Skala version, the only exceptions being the fortified towns which were able to remain on the coast.

Skala Eressou: located on the south coast towards the very western end of the island, Skala Eressou is another resort with a very fine beach. Many of the tavernas stand on wooden stilts on the edge of the beach creating a good dining atmosphere on summer evenings. Eressos was the birthplace of the poetess Sappho, regarded by many as the world's first recognised Lesbian. Although Eressos is trying hard to maintain the family image of the resort with considerable success, there are many lady visitors in summer who come to pay homage to Sappho. Skala Eressou and Sigri (below) are the resorts most distant from the airport.

Sigri: the most westerly resort on the island, Sigri is low key and natural. There is a harbour, small beaches, a village and castle to give it plenty of atmosphere.

Anaxos: this lovely family resort is located on the north coast. Away from the main road, it has a fine sandy beach and a good atmosphere.

Petra: also on the north coast and not too far east of Anaxos. Petra has a fine stretch of beach to offer sun worshippers with the lovely old village of Petra to explore.

Molyvos (Mythimna): this is the largest and most picturesque resort on the island. A castle guards the hilltop looking down on the village and harbour. Fascinating narrow streets on the hillside offer a different shopping experience while the harbour is just a great place to dine. Unfortunately, Molyvos also known as Mithymna, is not well blessed with beaches but there is one within walking distance to the east and those at Anaxos and Petra are a short taxi ride away. In summer a tourist boat ferries between Petra, Molyvos and Skala Sikaminias, outwards in the morning and returning late afternoon. There is also a bus connecting Anaxos, Petra, Molyvos and Eftalou in high season.

Thermi: located on the east coast just north of Mytilene town, Thermi is one of the oldest resorts on the island. Even so, it remains small and undeveloped by modern standards. People were attracted there originally for the hot springs and it is surrounded by relics from the earliest known settlements on the island. There is a sandy beach for relaxing and it makes an excellent base for exploring the eastern side of the island.

PEOPLE AND CULTURE

In spite of the many invaders over the centuries, the Greeks on Lesvos are openly friendly towards foreign visitors. It helps if you speak at least a little Greek but it does not matter too much. The Greeks do not seem to regard language as a barrier and will often chatter away in their native tongue in the full expectancy that you will understand some or part of whatever they are saying. Body language and gesticulations play a full part too.

LESVOS

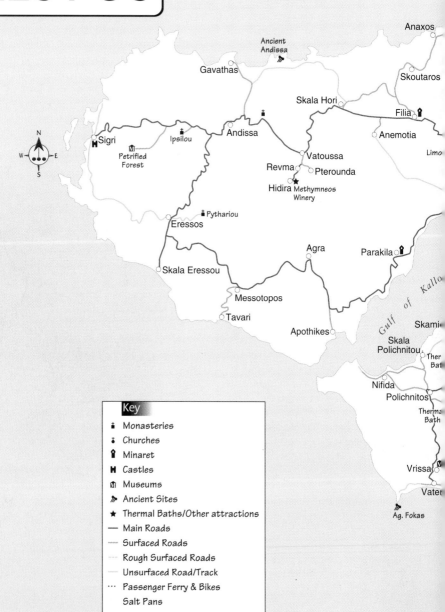

Anaxos

Ancient
Andissa

Gavathas

Skoutaros

Skala Hori

Filia

N

Sigri

Ipsilou

Andissa

Anemotia

W   E

Petrified
Forest

Vatoussa

Limo

Revma

Pterounda

S

Hidira Methymneos
Winery

Pythariou

Eressos

Agra

Parakila

Skala Eressou

of Kallo

Gulf

Messotopos

Tavari

Skami

Apothikes

Skala
Polichnitou

Ther
Bat

Nifida

Polichnitos

Therma
Bath

Key

    Monasteries

    Churches

    Minaret

    Castles

    Museums

    Ancient Sites

    Thermal Baths/Other attractions

—   Main Roads

—   Surfaced Roads

--- Rough Surfaced Roads

—   Unsurfaced Road/Track

··· Passenger Ferry & Bikes

     Salt Pans

Vrissa

Vater

Ag. Fokas

Komboloi; toys for boys

Usually a string of wood, plastic or metal beads, komboloi are the Greek's own form of worry beads used by men to relax from the stresses and strains of everyday life. It seems to be a preserve of men and women are rarely seen using them. Partially wrapped around the fingers, the beads are revolved in a flicking motion but there are several techniques of worrying which are surprisingly difficult to imitate for the untrained. Komboloi are thought to have developed from the Turkish rosary which has ninety nine pearls representing the names of Allah. This is clearly too unwieldy to use as a toy so the Greeks reduced the number to 13 or 15, or sometimes 17. For the Greeks it is a toy or a lucky charm and has no religious significance whatsoever.

The family unit is strong and still the basis of Greek society, although there are signs that the bonds are starting to weaken under western influences. It is sons who receive the adulation and are totally spoilt by their parents. This does not mean that daughters are not welcomed, as in some societies, and the ideal family is regarded as one son and one daughter. Parental influence is still strong when the time is right for their children to marry. Arranged marriages have not entirely disappeared. They are no longer the norm but parents still have a dominant role in satisfying the demands of society and tradition. It is the duty of the son to stand by his parents to ensure that suitable matches are made for all his sisters before he can contemplate marriage. Although a dowry is no longer a legal requirement, and this repeal was only in recent times, it is still perpetuated. A girl goes into marriage often with the gift of a furnished house or apartment from her parents. It remains the girls property and her security. In the same way gifts of gold for the bride, also to provide for her security, are not unusual. At least the newly wedded couple start life without the burden of debt and are able to build and plan a future for their own children. The family unit extends into business too. The Greek preference is for self employment or failing that a secure job with the state. Most small businesses employ only family and are eventually passed down via sons and daughters.

It is still a male dominated society but attitudes are slowly changing amongst the younger generation. Just a short time ago, only young men had the freedom to go out alone but this too has changed and young women are now part of the social scene. The role of women in the broader society has been recognised in legislation. They acquired the vote only in 1952 and the first woman Deputy was elected to Parliament the following year. Sexual discrimination in career opportunities and in the place of work has been outlawed. Many practical steps have been taken to assist the integration of women as equals in society. Low cost nurseries providing child places have been provided to free women to work and they have acquired rights of ownership after marriage and an equal share of communal property on divorce. Women now hold important posts in all branches of the Civil Service and in commerce but, in spite of all their progress, equality is only accepted in the big cities. Throughout rural Greece it remains contrary to the culture and fundamental change will only be fully accepted very slowly.

For women travelling alone on Lesvos there are no exceptional problems. The incidence of violent crime, including rape, is low, much lower than in other western societies. But it is not unknown and the same wariness of possible situations should be observed. Greek men firmly believe they are irresistible to all women so their attentions can be expected.

ECONOMY

For an island as large as Lesvos with a population of only 87,000 (1991), it is perhaps no surprise that farming is the mainstay of the economy. Olives are a major crop, a virtual monoculture, with 11 million trees cloaking the island (see Olive feature). Oil production fluctuates with the season, usually high every other season, but averages around 20,000 tonnes p.a.. Arable farming is limited to the areas of plain, notably around Kalloni at the head of the gulf.

Goats and sheep dominate livestock farming and they are widespread throughout, often in great flocks and herds. Goats are especially suited to the west of the island where the barren hillsides offer only sparse grazing. Cows are farmed too where there is sufficient grazing to support them.

Fishing is important but only on a local level. There are small ports all around the island, each supporting small fleets of individually owned boats. The fish is usually sold locally, from the quayside, to local tavernas or loaded into the back of a van to sell around the villages. The Greeks love their fish so there is always a ready market.

Olive culture makes a heavy demand on time only for a limited period in winter and early spring. This means that most farmers have another occupation, working in their own family business, running a shop or a taverna, working for the government or engaged in tourism.

Tourism too makes a significant contribution to the economy, although its full potential has yet to be realised.

FOOD AND DRINK

Watching the Greeks eat is a pleasure in itself. Seldom do they order individually, instead they order a vast number of communal dishes which fill the table to overflowing. They are far less concerned about cold food and many dishes which arrive hot are cold before they are eaten. Some tourists find it a bit disconcerting when their meals are actually served on the cool side but, in most areas, the message that tourists generally like their food hot has registered.

Above: Petra village *Above right:* Lady cutting faggots *Below:* Greek salad
Opposite left: Fish for sale *Opposite right:* Sun dried Octopus

Fast Food Greek Style

The Greeks are great nibblers, particularly in the mornings, so there is no shortage of fast-food. 'Pies' (pitta) with various fillings, usually made with filo pastry and looking like a Cornish pasty:-

Tiropitta: cheese. This is the most universally popular and found everywhere.

Spanakopitta: spinach only or with cheese and eggs.

Kreatopitta: minced meat.

Pizza: usually take-away small ones or sometimes sold as pieces.

Souvlaki: small pieces of meat on a wooden skewer served with a lump of bread or with pitta. Doner me pitta: slices of meat from the 'gyros' (meat cooked on a vertical spit) placed in a pitta parcel with a little yoghurt, tomato and onion.

Tost: usually a slice of ham and cheese toasted between bread.

and for the sweet tooth:-

Milopitta: apple.

Bougatza: vanilla custard.

Although the Greek cuisine is quite extensive, tavernas tend only to have a limited menu. Lunch time, between 2 and 3 o'clock after work finishes, is the only meal of the day for which the chef will prepare a range of cooked dishes. For the evening trade, and the Greeks are notoriously late eaters, the menu offers whatever is left over from lunch, which has often been kept warm for hours, and a range of grills which are cooked to order. Charcoal is generally used for grilling and it is not unusual to see large charcoal grills by the doorway or outside in summer.

MEZEDES

Menus usually offer a range of small dishes, known as mezedes, for starters. These include *tzatziki* (a yoghurt, cucumber and garlic dip), *taramasalata* (fish roe mixed with potato, oil and vinegar), *melitzano salata* (an aubergine dip with tomato and garlic) and *humus*, another dip this time from chickpeas. Fresh vegetables are rarely available but two vegetables which turn up as mezedes are *gigantes* (butter beans cooked in tomato and oil) and *arakas* (peas). *Saganaki*, fried cheese, is another interesting starter and *saganagi fournos*, a spicy cheese dish done in the oven, is usually on offer on Lesvos. The waiter will raise an eyebrow if mezedes are ordered separately by each individual. It is more fun to go Greek and order a selection of dishes to place on the table and share.

Salads may be preferred as starters or as part of the starters and the most popular is the village salad or *horiatiki salata* which may include lettuce, or cabbage, but less so now, tomato, onion, cucumber, peppers, *feta* cheese and olives. Tomatoes, cucumber, *feta* cheese and *maruli* (lettuce) are also offered as separate dishes.

MAIN COURSE

Ready cooked dishes may include the familiar *moussaka*, a mince dish with aubergines, potato and bechamel sauce, *kokanisto* (veal in tomato), *stifado* (veal stew with onions) or *giovetsi* (oven cooked lamb served with pasta). Chicken cooked on the spit is popular and inexpensive but favoured amongst the grills is souvlaki, veal or pork on a skewer. Chops, pork, lamb or veal, are ever present on the evening menus as are *keftedes* (spicy meat balls) and *bifteki* (mince burgers).

Fish is sometimes on offer but for a selection it is better to find a fish taverna, *psaria taverna*. Fish is becoming increasingly expensive and prices on the menu are often expressed per kilogram which makes them look sky high. In practice, a fish is weighed off and the charge is for that weight. A typical portion is around 400grm. *Astakos* (lobster) and *barbounia* (red mullet) are usually top of the menu and are expensive as are *garides* (shrimps). Octopus, grilled or cooked in wine is less expensive as is *kalamari* (squid). At the cheap end are *marides* (whitebait) which are eaten in their entirety, head and all. This dish is often available as a starter in a fish restaurant. Deserts are very limited, usually fruit, but the popularity of yoghurt and honey and creme caramel amongst tourists is now recognised. If you have tucked into your meal with obvious enjoyment, the proprietor may produce a plate of fruit, peeled and presented with his compliments.

DRINKS

Some Greeks prefer to drink ouzo with meals and this is served by the glass or small bottle and usually taken with water. Others choose retsina, a resinated wine, which is an acquired taste and the usual commercial brand is Kourtaki. Other brands, including Malamatina or Liokari, are less resinated and more widely appreciated. Most wine lists contain some of the countries acknowledged good wines like Boutari Naoussa as well as some medium priced popular ones like Kambas, Rotonda and Domestica. Limnos white wine is widely available on Lesvos and very popular. Try asking for '*spitiko krasi*' (house wine) which is usually served in a carafe or metal jug and can be very good.

FLORA AND FAUNA

Lesvos is especially rich in flowers and bird life. Spring is the best time for the flowers and with so many different habitats on the island, they are present in surprising variety. The orchid flora is particularly exciting with something like 70 species and subspecies recorded over the years. The best months for the flowers is March, April and early May. For the number and variety of orchids, the end of March and early April is the peak. The wild *Paeonia mascula* grows in the Agiassos area as does

the beautiful *Fritillaria pontica*. Once physically part of Asia Minor, it is not surprising the Lesvos flora has strong associations with Turkey. One fine excellent example of this is *Rhododendron lutea* which has a foothold on Lesvos in the mountains west of Kalloni.

Theophrastus, Father of Botany

Theophrastus was born in Eressos around 372BC and became one of the greatest of the early philosophers. He studied in Athens under Aristotle and, when Aristotle retired, Theophrastus became head of the Lyceum, the academy founded by Aristotle.

During a long life, he was around 85 when he died, Theophrastus wrote about 200 treatises on different subjects. Two of the few surviving works are related to plants, 'Inquiry into Plants' running to nine books and 'Growth of Plants' running to six.

His work on plants was wide ranging and embraces a wide view of the vegetable kingdom. Trees and different kinds of timber are explored, shrubs, thorny bushes, gums from trees, ornamental plants and kitchen and garden plants.

There must have been something special about Eressos since this was also the birthplace of the poetess Sappho, although more than 200 years earlier.

Walking through olive groves

Above left: The toothed orchid, *Orchis tridentata* *Above right:* Pink butterfly orchid, *Orchis papilionaceae* *Below:* Balkan white butterflies on a thistle

The birds on Lesvos are every bit as spectacular as the flowers. The island lies on an important migration route and offers the birds a wide variety of habitats, especially wetlands, where the birds can rest, feed and gather strength for their onward journeys. Most of the important wetlands surround the Gulf of Kalloni, the salt pans at Skala Polichnitou and at Kalloni, the rivers in the area, the marshes near Parakila and the pool by the beach at Skala Kallonis. Some of the birds which can be seen on the island include white storks, black-winged stilts, squacco herons, purple herons, whiskered terns and collared pratincoles but the full list extends to over 300.

As on most Greek islands, the hunters keep down numbers of the larger mammals but there are plenty of Persian squirrels around. This particular squirrel seems to have a habit of racing along in front of the car on country roads and leaping aside at the last moment! There are foxes, beech martins, brown hares and otters but these are rarely seen by casual visitors.

There are plenty of reptiles and anyone spending a little time in the countryside has a chance of seeing a spur-thighed tortoise or hear the knocking of shells during the spring mating ritual. Two terrapins are commonly seen on the island, the stripe-necked terrapin and the European pond terrapin and a whole selection of lizards including the agama lizard and the Balkan green. Snakes are around in variety but are hardly ever a problem. It pays to be aware that some, like the montpellier snake, are poisonous, although this species has rear fangs which makes it difficult for it to bite humans, unless handled.

Butterflies are one of the delights of the island and there are plenty to see and, if you are lucky, photograph. Some to watch out for include the swallowtail, eastern festoon, orange tip, clouded yellow, Cleopatra and painted lady.

ARTS AND CRAFTS

Pottery remains the most important of the crafts practised on Lesvos and has been since ancient times. Most of the productive potters are now found in Agiassos. Lesvos pottery is distinctive and character-ised by bright bold colours. Wood carving too is another skill found on the island and again centred around Agiassos but can be found anywhere on the island.

HISTORY

Situated near the Hellespont (now Dardanelles) trade routes, Lesvos has throughout history been of strategic and commercial import-ance. This placed it constantly under threat from opposing forces of the east and west leaving it with a story of turbulence to tell from ancient to modern times.

There might have been more chapters of history written had earthquakes not destroyed so much evidence from the ancient cities and if more archaeological excavations had been carried out on the island. Thermi, just north of Mytilene town, is the area which has been most studied and there is evidence from there of prehistoric settlements as early as the third millennium BC thought to be associated with people from Troy. These probably existed throughout the times of the Minoans and Myceneans.

THE EMERGENCE OF CITIES

The population of Lesvos started to increase from around 1200BC or even earlier by migrant tribes from other regions, from the Peloponnese, the Argolid and Thesally, which led to settlements developing all over the island. Five of these grew into important City States, Mytilene, Mythimna (Molyvos), Eressos, Pyrrha and Antissa, as did a sixth, Arisbe, but this was later destroyed by earthquakes. Mytilene, originally built on an island which was eventually joined to the mainland by a causeway, became the largest and most important of these cities and for a time extensively colonised the opposite shores of Asia Minor.

Political upheaval and friction between these cities led to the building of fortifications around the 8th century BC but eventually a settled age developed, especially under the leadership of Pittakos (650 BC - ca570), now regarded as one of the seven sages of antiquity. Lesvos rose to prominence in this period and became a power in the region. The arts flourished too and some of the greatest poets of the age came to prominence, names which are now firmly written in history, notably Sappho and Alcaeus.

TROUBLED TIMES

The whole of the region now known as Greece was caught up in wars which carried on for over 200 years. Lesvos was an early casualty in the Greco-Persian Wars (c. 546-c. 448 BC), and fell to the Persians around 520BC and was not liberated until 479BC with the defeat of the Persian naval forces. The island then joined the Delian League supported by Athens while the Peloponnese formed their own league in opposition. A full scale war started between these two major powers in 431BC and Lesvos attempted to defect from Athens to join Sparta but was severely put down by Athens. In 405BC it was eventually captured by Sparta but by 389BC it was back under Athenian domination. Caught up in the Corinthian War (395-387 BC), the island was again captured by Sparta but returned to Athens in a second Athenian Alliance around 375BC.

PEACE AND PROSPERITY

Lesvos had strongly supported Philip of Macedon in the anti-Persian Confederacy (338BC) but was besieged and captured by the Persian fleet under Memnon of Rhodes in 333BC for its trouble. Alexander the Great was quick to liberate Lesvos and restore its territories on Asia Minor. A period of relative prosperity followed and the island grew in affluence. For a time Mytilene rivalled in splendour other great cities like Rhodes and Ephesus. The expansion of the Roman empire started around 200BC and Lesvos was again caught up in the conflict, siding first with Rome but eventually being attacked by Antiochus III from the Hellenic civilisation in Syria. Finally, Lesvos came under the control of Rome.

ROMAN LESVOS (88BC - AD324)

When peace settled again, Mytilene was granted many privileges by Rome and a treaty of friendship drafted in 24BC. The town of Mytilene developed into the island's capital, the once great city of Antissa, destroyed by the Romans in 168BC, was now merely a village under the control of Mythimna and Pyrrha had declined. The autonomy of the cities was lost when Vespasian (AD67-69) declared Mytilene a Roman province. The situation turned around in AD124 when Hadrian came to power. Good relations with Rome were restored and it was in this period that the huge aqueduct carrying water from Mount Olympos to Mytilene was built. Parts of this can still be seen at Moria and Lambou Mili.

Christianity did not spread to Lesvos until sometime around the second century. The island had been wedded to the worship of the *Dodecatheon* and the cult of emperors. It was in this sort of climate that St Paul dropped anchor on Lesvos on his third apostolic journey in the spring of AD58.

Above and opposite top: Mytilene castle *Opposite bottom:* Ag. Isidoros beach

The Great Icon Controversy

Although in the early church the making and veneration of portraits of Christ and the saints was consistently opposed. The use of icons, nevertheless, gained popularity especially in the eastern provinces of the Roman Empire. By the 7th century it had become an officially encouraged cult. Opposition to this practice by the iconoclasts started to fester and it blew up into a huge dispute in the 8th and 9th centuries.

Byzantine emperor Leo III took a public stand against icons in 726 and in 730 their use was officially prohibited. Now with the upper hand, the iconoclasts started a persecution of the icon worshippers which was to last for more than 50 years throughout the reign of emperor Constantine V.

In 787 Emperor Irene convened the seventh ecumenical council at Nicaea and successfully argued for their return but icons were banned again (815) with Leo V's ascension. Eventually, in 843, Theodora, the widow of emperor Theophilus, finally and forever restored icon veneration. This event is now celebrated on the first Sunday in Lent in Greece as the Feast of Orthodoxy.

The emperor Irene, who reigned first as empress and finally as emperor, led a life of intrigue and conspiracy to keep herself in power. Eventually she was exiled to Lesvos and died there in 803 but her zeal in working towards the restoration of icons gained her recognition as a saint in the Greek Orthodox Church. Her feast day is August 9th.

BYZANTINE LESVOS

On the division of the Roman Empire in AD286, Lesvos was included in the *Provincia Insularum* of the eastern state. A new rural character started to develop over the following centuries and the beginning of internal development accompanied by a decline in urban populations. This came about with the increase of piracy restricting sea trade which had been the main source of prosperity.

THE LOST CENTURIES

From the lack of detail in recorded history, it seems that Lesvos had no significant role in the events of the region over many centuries. That is not to say that it was left in peace. The island was sacked by 400 Vandals, prisoners of General Belisarios, in 534 which is thought to have encouraged the town of Mytilene to strengthen its defences.

Later, in 821 Lesvos was captured by the mercenary hordes of Thomas the Slav and used as a base for plundering the region. It brought reprisals from the Saracens over several decades.

Invaders ebbed and flowed over the next few centuries until they were caught up in the momentous events when Constantinople fell to the Venetians and crusaders in the Fourth Crusade of 1204. Lesvos was allotted to the Count of Flanders who was also elected emperor as Baldwin I. As in other parts, the churches and monasteries were plundered and the goods and properties shared out amongst the Latin clergy and nobles. In 1354 the island was given to a Genoese trading family.

THE TURKISH OCCUPATION (1462 -1911)

The violent incorporation of Lesvos into the expanding Ottoman Empire affected the island economically and politically for centuries. Again the monasteries and churches suffered and a large part of the population either moved inland or were shipped off to Constantinople. The Ottomans fearing that Lesvos was too good a staging post for western attacks, effectively closed down its maritime trade and encouraged farming as the main occupation.

All attempts to recover the island for the west, and there were many in the 16th century, usually ended with some part of the island being sacked. The Turks responded by rebuilding and strengthening the castles and occupying more of the shoreline. Settlements moved inland and even today only the fortified towns occupy coastal positions, such as Mytilene and Molyvos, whereas other towns are situated about 2-3 miles (3-5 kms) inland. There are many examples of these, Polichnitos, Kalloni, Moria and Thermi to name a few.

By the end of the 16th century, things were much quieter and Ottomans from the mainland started to settle on the island. The Turkish officials and the military became the guardians of law and order and tax collectors. Land was divided and ceded with deeds or leases to individuals with a tax on the revenue it generated. Over the centuries the right to use land turned eventually into ownership. Olive plantations started to proliferate, especially in the east and south of the island, and olive oil was destined to be an important product in the 18th century.

Lesvos was eventually liberated from the Turks in 1912 and officially annexed to Greece in 1923 with the signing of the Treaty of Lausanne.

2 Out & About

GOOD BEACH GUIDE

A day out on a different beach provides a refreshing change and the purpose of this guide is to help with choices. There are a good number of beaches around the island, large and small but this is not intended to be a comprehensive list. It includes only those beaches with good features which reward the effort of getting there. Sandy beaches are selected in the main but outstandingly good shingle beaches are also included. Most beaches on the island, with the possible exception of Eftalou and Ag. Ermogenis, have easy access for wheelchairs and prams.

Opposite page: Barren landscape of the west, near Mesotopos
Right: Skala Sikaminias Harbour
Below: Beach south of Sigri

Refer to the map of the island for locations. For ease of reference they are listed in clockwise order starting from Ag. Ermogenis due south of Mytilene town near the entrance to the Gulf of Gera. Further details of some of these beaches and the resorts may be found by consulting the car tours.

AG. ERMOGENIS

A tiny picturesque bay overlooked by a white church and a taverna. The beach area is quite small so it can easily become crowded. It is within easy reach of Mytilene so expect the locals to be there in numbers at the weekend.

AG. ISIDOROS

There is a long, long beach of fine sand to enjoy here with tavernas close by for refreshments. Head for the eastern side of this beach, away from the main road, to find the most popular part with the best services.

VATERA

Some 5 miles (8km) of excellent quality sand in a wide and peaceful bay. There is plenty of space here to find your own quiet spot. There are bars and tavernas strung along the road behind the beach so refreshments are never too far away. Sun loungers and umbrellas provided by the hotels are on a pay basis but the tavernas do not normally charge their customers.

Free showers, changing booths, nets for beach volleyball are provided as well as some small areas set aside for children's playgrounds.

Water sports are catered for at two locations so prepare to water ski, windsurf, canoe, ride a banana, a donut or paddle more sedately in a pedalo.

SKALA KALLONIS

Nicely situated at the head of the Gulf of Kallonis, Skala Kallonis has two fine beaches, one either side of the small fishing port. Both are well furnished with sun loungers and shades. Leave your sun lounger at your peril, the local pelican lies in wait to settle himself on any vacant chair that looks comfortable. The sea here is shallow for a reasonable distance from the shore which provides safer bathing for children and non swimmers. Water sports facilities are available as are beach showers and changing cubicles.

SKALA ERESSOU

There is no need to be up early to grab a spot on this beach with over 1.5 miles (2.5km) of golden sands spreading across the whole resort. Great for swimmers as the beach shelves steeply into the sea but keep on eye on the children. Laze around on a pedalo or energise with the active water sports available. Loads of beach side tavernas in the central area and loads of privacy either side. All the usual beach furniture is available.

SIGRI

There are a couple of reasonable beaches at Sigri but neither very big. Activities here are much more low key.

ANAXOS

The beach, like the resort, is tucked away off the main road and confusing to access by car. A dark, sandy beach awaits which is surprisingly large. Refreshments and ice cream are close at hand and water sports are available in season.

PETRA

A long stretch of sandy beach, narrow near the village but deeper on the Molyvos side. Sunbeds, showers, changing huts, water sports and even a tennis court. With plenty of tavernas on hand, refreshments are never too far away.

EFTALOU

Fine shingle beach just east of Molyvos which is reached by actually walking through the entrance of the hot springs bath house. Apart from changing huts and showers, there are few facilities but, be warned, this rather private beach was popular with nude bathers in the past although less so these days. There is a taverna further along the beach which is open in season.

THERMI

Running south from the harbour, it starts as a narrow strip and gradually widens. Most of the facilities are provided by the hotels which back onto the beach.

A DAY OUT IN MYTILENE TOWN

The first glimpse of Mytilene town for visitors is on the drive from the airport out to their resort. Unfortunately, the route through the town shows the very worst aspects, overcrowded narrow roads, shabby buildings and uninspiring shops. This poor image often deters people from returning to explore the town. This is far from the truth, it is an exciting place with so much to enjoy.

HIGHLIGHTS

- pedestrianised Ermou street for shopping
- castle
- excellent archaeological museums
- Byzantine museum
- Ancient theatre
- Turkish mosque
- Fine architecture
- Sea front promenade

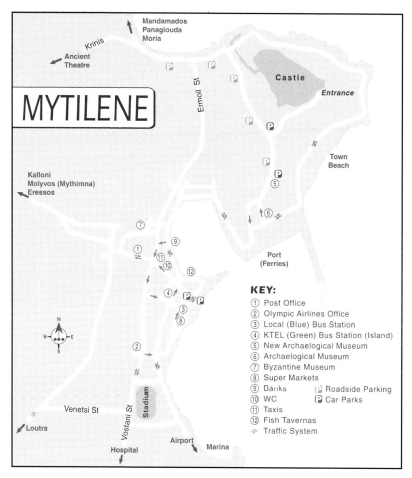

Although this is a large town with around 25,000 residents, almost a third of the island's population, which spreads up the surrounding hillsides, the places of interest are confined to a small area in the old part close to the sea front. All of them can be reached on foot and this tour will nicely fill a morning. Morning is the best time since most shops and museums close in the afternoons.

Narrow streets and parking problems tend to put off many visitors from visiting by car. There is a large car park south of the city near the sea front but the easiest option is to approach the city from the north and park near the castle. This is too far out of town for most of the Greeks but convenient for a circular tour on foot.

All the approaches to Mytilene from the west eventually pass around the top of the Gulf of Gera. Look here for the road off left to Moria and follow this to reach the coast road and turn southward

Above left: Mytilene castle *Above right:* Mytilene has many fine mansion houses and buildings, like the one shown, which were built around the beginning of the 19th century

towards Mytilene town. This entrance to town leads through a run down industrial section which surrounds the old north harbour. Watch out for the sight of an old Turkish baths on the seaward side. Find a parking place just before reaching the castle or continue inland alongside the castle to park by the roadside or in the car park of the Archaeological Museum.

Head for the castle to start the tour, the entrance is accessed from the narrow road just before the Archaeological Museum. Back in the 5th century BC, the castle area occupied a small island isolated from the main island by a narrow stretch of water. This was the site of the original Mytilene town with the acropolis and oldest part built on the highest ground. Even in those times the city extended on to mainland Lesvos. Fortification took place in stages as Mytilene became embroiled in struggles through the centuries. In 1260 it was listed by Venetians as one of the most strongly fortified forts in the eastern Mediterranean. A century later it was almost completely rebuilt and further strengthened by the Genoan Francesco Gattelusi. He was the brother-in-law of the Emperor and had been given Lesvos in return for services rendered. On

Sept. 1st 1462 the fort was besieged by the Turks who at first suffered heavy losses. They brought up six pieces of heavy ordnance and fired relentlessly wreaking terrible damage on the castle. The Greeks survived this for two weeks before capitulating.

Less of the castle remains now than in its heyday, but there are walls and buildings to see including the palace of Francesco Gattelusi. The grounds of the castle are honeycombed with underground tunnels used as safe shelters. It is an evocative place just to stand and imagine those galleons standing out at sea with their cannons run out.

Leave the castle area and return to the main road, 8th November. Follow left to reach the new Archaeological Museum very shortly, open 8am-2pm, closed Monday.

Built in 1995, this museum attempts to depict life on Lesvos from the second century BC to the third century AD. Domestic utensils and every day objects are displayed as well as statues of religious or symbolic character. One of the highlights of this museum is the stunning mosaics which are beautifully displayed throughout Galleries I, II and VI. Apart from the more usual lions and fish, the mosaics in Gallery I depicting scenes from Menander's comedies are especially absorbing. This museum is worth visiting for the mosaics alone which rank amongst the finest.

Below: Mytilene waterfront showing the dome of Ag. Therapon

MENANDER CA 342BC - CA292BC

Menander was an Athenian dramatist, a pre-eminent exponent of New Comedy, effectively the last flowering of Athenian stage comedy. He wrote more than 100 plays but only eight brought him victory at Athenian dramatic festivals.

Known facts about his life are few but he was a pupil of Theophrastus and probably lived in Athens for most of his life. His skill at comedy was deft, using fictitious characters from ordinary life to create reality. His work was adapted by Roman writers and through them influenced European comedy from the Renaissance.

There is no suggestion that he lived on Lesvos but one of the Roman villas excavated near the ancient theatre became known as 'Menander's house' because of the mosaics found there relating to characters in his plays.

A ticket for the new museum also includes entrance to the old museum, the Museum of Mytilene, which is very different and should not be missed. It is housed in a nearby 1912 mansion which once belonged to the family of Achilleas Vournazos.

Leave the new museum and turn left to continue along 8th November road. Stay left at the fork, still following 8th November, and the old museum is on the left at the bottom corner. This museum gives a wider view of the history of Lesvos starting with artefacts from prehistoric sites on the island and tracing a timeline through the Bronze age, the Classical and Roman periods right through to Medieval Lesvos. The gold jewellery from Hellenistic times onward in Gallery VII is something to look out for. There is a good collection of heavier pieces, capitals, funeral stelai and similar on display, some in the outside courtyard. It is an excellent introduction to the history of the island.

Carry on from the old museum with the sea, or rather the ferry port, on your left and head towards the 'new south' harbour. The north harbour was the focus of commerce and seafaring for Mytilene until the mid-19th century. This all changed when the new south harbour was constructed. Its promenade on the seaward side offers easier walking around the harbour, especially since pavement cafés fill the whole of the pavement in places on the landward side. Anyway, the city skyline is more dramatic looking from the promenade. Especially dominant is the lovely dome of the church of Ag. Therapon which is visited on the return route. There is a statue of the famous poetess Sappho in glistening white marble on the inland side. All the best fish restaurants are located across on the far side of the harbour where a mole leads out to a beacon. This is where the Mytilinians themselves love to dine.

Having walked almost two sides of the harbour, cross to the landward side and take the short road inland signposted Kalloni.

The statue of the Sappho, the island's famous poetess

This roads leads to the start of the pedestrianised Ermou shopping street where you turn right. On our first acquaintance with Ermou back in 1985, it was full of dusty shops selling little more than bric-a-brac. It has had a make-over since then and is now full of sophisticated shops selling many of the goods on sale in modern European capitals. There are still plenty of shops selling more domestic items, including fish stalls spilling out into the street, hardware shops and street sellers offering dried herbs. Much of the sophistication is lost as you proceed to the far end where dusty old junk shops and antique shops have more of a presence.

Before making too much progress down Ermou, turn left to visit Ag. Therapon and the Byzantine museum next door. The museum offers a collection of important icons, sections of beautifully carved old iconostases and the usual church vestments. The church itself is typical Greek Orthodox.

Return to Ermou to continue where, centuries earlier, you would have been walking on water. This road follows the route of the channel which separated the island containing the old city from the mainland. It is a street full of character and interest, not to mention the odd motorbike even though it is pedestrianised. As you leave the main shops behind to reach the less commercial part, look out for the old Turkish mosque, Yeni Cami, on the right. Keep going re-lentlessly along Ermou to emerge back in north harbour, not too far from where the car is parked.

There is still a diversion remaining by car, if you wish to see the old theatre. Head north on reaching the coast road and look for Krinis street on the left. This leads steeply uphill through several cross-roads, turn left at the third of these. Follow as the road bends right then turn left and park in a clearing opposite a cemetery. Head for the pine trees and take the right upward fork to reach the ancient theatre. The gate is unlocked. This theatre, like others of the same era, enjoyed breathtaking views. It was excavated as late as 1958 by D. Evangelidis who suggested its seating capacity might have been as high as 15,000. It dates originally from the Hellenistic period but was renovated in the Roman period. It is likely that many of the stones were removed for other local projects, including the renovation of the castle by Gattelusi in the 14th century. All that remains is the shape of the theatre on the hillside, the orchestra and parts of the stage. To the west of the theatre, near the Ag. Kyriaki graveyard, there are some remains of the ancient polygonal wall of ancient Mytilene town.

Island Hopping

Lesvos is very much at the end of a branch line when it comes to island hopping. It is well connected to Athens (Piraeus) via Chios and to Thessaloniki via Limnos and also to Kavala on the northern mainland, again via Limnos. The sailing time from Lesvos to Piraeus is 12 hours but there is a faster boat taking half the time.

It can seem like hard work to get into the mainstream circuit of islands from Lesvos but it is not really difficult. There are moves to improve inter-island connections but ferry boat services and timetables in Greece are not written in tablets of stone. They can and do change at whim. During the summer there is a ferry boat running weekly which sails down from Thessaloniki through Lesvos, Chios, Samos, Rhodes and onto Crete. Samos has fairly frequent connections with the Cyclades so it is possible to hop off there and head off to Naxos and from there the islands are your playground. There is also a hydrofoil service to Samos.

Another option for getting to Samos is to take the regular Athens ferry, hop off at Chios and take the small ferry which runs down to Samos on several days each week. Check connection days for an uninterrupted journey or be prepared to explore Chios for a day or two while waiting.

Ferries depart from the port in Mytilene but there are ferry boats in summer from Sigri which connect with Limnos and Kavala or Limnos and Rafina.

If you prefer to travel in the fast lane, there is a scheduled flight between Rhodes and Thessaloniki stopping *en route* on Samos, Chios, Mytilene and Limnos.

Opposite top: Octopus drying in the sun, Molyvos harbour
Opposite bottom: Molyvos harbour

A DAY OUT IN MOLYVOS

Molyvos, like Mytilene, developed around a fortified acropolis. Whereas Mytilene developed into the capital, Molyvos declined in importance. Molyvos scores in that it is much more picturesque and has developed into the most attractive tourist resort on the island. The light of day is the best time for exploration but the atmosphere on those warm evenings when the castle is floodlit is something which has to be experienced.

HIGHLIGHTS

- The castle
- Harbour
- Shopping
- Character streets

The ancient name of Mithymna was in use for many centuries, until the Middle Ages. The Turks renamed the town Molyvos and so it stayed until 1912. After the liberation of the island from the Turks, the residents reverted to its former name but not fully so both names remain in current use. In tourist terms, the town is best known as Molyvos. Mithymna (or Methymna) is derived from a Pelasgian, pre Hellenic culture, word meaning protected.

Mithymna; fact or fiction

The first Greeks to arrive on Lesvos came after the Trojan war around the 11th century BC. They were Aeolian tribes from the Peloponnese and Boeotia and built beautiful cities including the one here at Mithymna. They built a harbour and a fortified acropolis. One of the first Aeolian settlers was Makar with his daughters, amongst whom were Mithymna and Mytilene. Their names were given to the cities. Other legends say that Mithymna was the wife of Makar and even she was wife and daughter.

The highest mountain behind Mithymna, Mt Lepetimnos, was named by the hero Lepetimnos who married Mithymna during the Trojan war. An altar was built on top of the mountain to honour Lepetimnos. The ancients also believe that Achilles and Ajax brought the body of Palamedes, another hero of the Trojan war, to lay to rest by the altar on the mountain top.

The location of Molyvos was ideal for early settlement, an easily defended hill, a place to make a harbour and easy land to cultivate immediately adjacent. It could hardly have been more perfect. It was able to support a good population and there is plenty of archaeological evidence to suggest the ancient city covered a much wider area than the modern town. The boundaries of the ancient city changed with time but originally it spread over the headland to the west, above the harbour, and to the north.

In ancient times, there was great rivalry between Mithymna and Mytilene. Mithymna followed policies opposite to those of the first city so, while Mytilene was friendly with the Athenians, Mithymna hated them. Nevertheless, they shared a similar history to Mytilene in capture and release over the centuries. The Middle Ages were a particularly bad time for Molyvos. Their exposed position on the north coast left them open to attack from any passing raiders, and they were raided frequently by the Arabs, the Venetians and the Turks.

Arriving by car, park in the large car park on the approach to Molyvos. Out of season it is possible to drive a little further in but there is little car parking space and it quickly gets congested. The approach to Molyvos gives one of the best views of the town with the castle crowning the top of the hill and the closely packed houses jostling for position down the hillside below.

Molyvos Bird Life

It is not unusual to see people standing in one or all of the lay-bys on the approach to Molyvos, peering at the hillside through binoculars. It is one of the best sites on the island for spotting Ruppell's warbler but equally good for peregrine falcons and the spectacular blue rock thrush.

This walking tour leads first down to the harbour, returning back up the hill then working up the narrow streets to visit the castle. From the car park walk into Molyvos along the coastal road to take in the views and notice the very narrow strip of beach below. There are far better beaches close by, either south of the town at Petra or along the north coast to the east at Eftalou.

One or two of the alleyways off left lead down to cafés and to the shore. Very shortly, the road leads in descent down to the harbour area. Surrounded by tavernas, and frequently hung with octopus drying in the sun, this is an enticing place to think about lunch or perhaps a cold beer. There are one or two excellent craft shops in the harbour area, selling unusual craft work of a high standard.

Leave the harbour to head back up the hill and, once over the crown, fork left up the cobbled street. After a short climb this takes you wandering into the arterial market street, the magical heart of the old village. Little shops crowd the shaded street, a real mix of local fruit and vegetables and tourist souvenir shops. The gold shops are particularly good and worth a second look. This arterial road rises gently through the contours of the hill but to get to the castle, you will need to continue up right when the cluster of shops is left behind. The route twists and turns through a few right angles but eventually, it will bring you up to the summit and the castle.

Alcaeus (ca 620BC - ca580BC)

Alcaeus, the son of an aristocratic family, was born in Mythimna. He was a contemporary of Sappho of Eressos. Like Sappho, he was a lyric poet whose work was highly regarded in the ancient world. The only fragments of his poems remaining show the quality and range of his interests. He was also a politician so, perhaps not surprisingly, his work often dwelt on the political life of the times but his poems covered the much wider themes of love, ships, countryside and the atmosphere of everyday life.

The castle, or rather fort, as it now stands is Medieval rebuilt in the Byzantine period but further strengthened in 1354 by the Genoan Francesco Gattelusi, brother-in-law of the Emperor. This parallels the events at the fortress at Mytilene. The gateway and walls at Molyvos have survived in remarkably good condition and although there is little to see inside,

Molyvos castle and town

except for spectacular views down from the ramparts. Its potential for holding concerts became reality with some renovations in the nineties and there is also a small artist's studio tucked away inside.

There are two routes back to the car from here, either you can wander back through the alleyways down through the old town to the coast road or, follow the main road from the castle entrance winding down the back of the hill.

A DAY OUT IN AGIASSOS (AYIASSOS)

Built on the north east slopes of Mount Olympos, Agiassos, at an elevation rising from 1300ft (400m), is the highest inhabited town on the island.

HIGHLIGHTS INCLUDE

- The ambience and the old character of this hill town
- The agora street
- Church of the Virgin Mary of Agiassos
- The beauty of the location

The easiest approach to Agiassos is from the Mytilene - Polichnitos road. It is impossible not to admire the olive groves here with the lovely, old gnarled tree trunks beneath those silvery grey leaves. Life in these parts is dedicated to the farming of olives and the production of olive oil. In the tavernas, it is one topic of conversation that remains ceaseless amongst the men. In spring the flowers in these olive groves are spectacular, passing through phases with the season.

Anemones provide the early display in shades of mauve, pink and red. Lesvos has a brilliant red *Anemone pavonina*, not seen on many other islands. Yellow chrysanthemums too sometimes swathe whole groves. Red poppies eventually replace the anemones and the chrysanthemums as the season progresses.

The trouble with 'g'

Many visitors experience considerable difficulties with the Greek alphabet and language. Even though many signs are transliterated into the Latin alphabet, it is still not easy to get the pronunciation correct without understanding some of the basic rules. The letter g is one that seems to cause most problems, mainly because it crops up in one frequently used word, *Agios*, meaning saint, which is used in many church and place names.

The rules of pronunciation for this letter are quite simple. If g is followed by e or i it is pronounced as a y, otherwise it remains g. So *Agiassos* is pronounced Ayiassos and the word for saint, Ayios or Ayia for a lady.

Below: Souvenirs and fruit shop, Agiassos

Parking in Agiassos is something of a problem so park on reaching the town itself, before the bus station and prepare to walk. Everything is uphill from here since this is the lowest part of town. There are tavernas on hand if you feel ready for refreshments but there are still more in the town. Walk up the main street, passing a number of souvenir shops, many of which are rich in religious artefacts to cater for religious tourism. Keep left all the time to reach the wisteria decked streets surrounding the church. All life is here, men sitting out at tables, women crowding into the mouth watering bread shop, a favourite for visitors too, or looking at the wide selection of cheeses in the cheese shop. This is the heart of this surprisingly large town and it is all centred around the church.

tip: try here one of the island's traditional cheeses, *ladotiri*, a hard cheese which is allowed to mature submerged in olive oil. It is delicious and very easy to become a convert.

The church of Agiassos, dedicated to the Virgin Mary, is the most important on the island, attracting religious tourists from all over Greece. It is the custodian of Greek Orthodoxy on the island and vitally important to the town. Built originally in 1170, the present church dates from 1814. The huge attraction which draws modern pilgrims to the island to visit this church in particular is the miracle-working icon of Mary with Infant. Legend tells that it is the work of St Luke and was brought to the island from Jerusalem in AD 803 by Agathon of Ephesus. This was in the period when Emperor Irene had argued successfully to restore the use of icons but they were banned again later for a time (see The Great Icon Controversy). It is hard not to be moved by the awe-inspiring interior of this beautiful Byzantine church or marvel at the sumptuously gilded iconostasis.

The saint's day of Our Lady of Agiassos is August 15th and is shared by every Maria in Greece. It is a particularly huge festival on Lesvos and centred here in Agiassos. It starts on August 1st when many pilgrims come and take up residence in the cell-like rooms surrounding the courtyard and remain for the full fifteen days. Others walk to the church, many following an old route from Karini, but the day itself is a mega event in Agiassos. After mass, the icon is carried around the town in a solemn parade.

Fascinating to photographers and artists are narrow streets of closely packed houses which rise away from the church up the steep hillsides. Shoppers will prefer to concentrate on the lower part of town looking for bargains amongst the colourful pottery, the best place on the island for this, and the wood carvings.

Agiassos is surrounded by some of the island's most beautiful countryside. The surrounding mountains are forested with chestnut and pine trees but there are farms of olive, cherry and apple trees. It offers superb walking and there are many tracks and trails to follow which give a full flavour of the region. A couple of walking suggestions are included here but for more information see Walking in the Fact File.

Walk no 1: The Pilgrims' Way

This walk follows an old cobbled trail which connects Agiassos with Karini and is used by many to walk up to the church in Agiassos on August 15th. It can be done in either direction but here we are following in the footsteps of the pilgrims. The distance up to the church from the starting point is around 3.5 miles (5.5km); allow about least 3 hours return and be sure to carry some water.

Karini lies on the main road between Mytilene and Polichnitos almost due north of Agiassos. Park the car in the region of the two tavernas which lie opposite. The taverna on the north side is very leafy, almost hidden amongst plane trees. Cross the road from this taverna and take a path beside an old olive oil factory. Behind the factory, the path joins an old cobbled trail where you follow it uphill. The trail is a bit disrupted early on with cobbles missing and some sections have been newly repaired.

There is no more route finding as this lovely old trail leads directly uphill into Agiassos. There is a diversion that can be taken to visit the old village of Asomatos, where, if it is before lunch, you might find a taverna open for a drink or you may not! For Asomatos, turn left where a road crosses the trail. Return to this point to carry on up to Agiassos.

Olive groves bound either side of the track as you continue to rise. Signs of habitation indicate that Agiassos is very close and, once under the road bridge, you emerge at the very top of the town. Carry on straight downhill from here to the centre of town for the church.

Walk No2: The Byzantine Kasteli

The Kasteli stands very noticeably on top of a small peak just north of the town and is easily seen as you drive into Agiassos. This is the site of an old castle but is now occupied by a church. The walk to get there and back is quite short, 2.5 miles (4km) in its entirety and takes just over an hour for the return trip.

Start at the bus station and walk away from the town. In around 5 minutes, watch out for a trail on the left, just after the fire station, sign posted Kasteli. Turn up this trail and prepare to turn sharp left in around a further 10 minutes, ignoring the trail ahead. Continue to climb steadily on what becomes a fine cobbled trail to reach the church in around 30 minutes or so. Enjoy the views and return the same way.

CAR TOURS

Lesvos is a large island with many places of interest. Coach tours are so very limited and the convoluted shape of Lesvos does not allow for the ever-popular round-the-island type of tour. Easily the most rewarding and satisfying way to discover Lesvos is by car. These tours are designed to take in the highlights of the island with some off-the-beaten track places that the casual visitor might easily miss. It is best not to attempt to drive hire cars on mountain roads shown as scenic on the map unless with prior knowledge of the state of the track. (See Car Hire) Most are only suitable for 4WD vehicles.

Skala Kallonis has been chosen as a starting place for all the tours described below. Located at the hub of the island, it is a very central location and visitors staying elsewhere will not find it difficult to join in the tours.

Only Mytilene town suffers from traffic congestion. Roads on the rest of the island are generally free flowing. Most road surfaces are good but be aware that pot holes often develop over winter which take some time to get repaired. Distances may seem short but the roads wind and twist, especially in the west, and can be slow to drive. Outstandingly the best map for the island is the Road Edition, 1:70,000 Lesvos no 212. It is the most reliable and accurate map available, except for an error which may cause confusion on Car Tour 1. The road from Kalloni westward through Filia to Skalahori is the main road and not a secondary road as shown.

The road from Skalahori to Skoutaros is a fairly new road.

CAR TOUR 1: THE WILD WEST

Torrents of volcanic lava poured over the western end of the island some 20 million years ago turning the forests into stone and the land into a moonscape. Dramatic landscapes, unique on this island, a petrified forest and two resorts, Eressos, the birthplace of Sappho, and Sigri provide the backbone of this 87 mile (140km) day long tour.

The sweeping beach at Skala Kallonis might stop you in your tracks before the tour even starts. If that is not arresting enough, the large pool behind the beach might well be, especially if you are a bird watcher. Throughout the winter months right into late May, until the pool effectively dries up, it is teeming with bird life. The list of species is appetising and includes the very elegant black-winged stilt, the squacco heron, glossy ibis and the purple heron amongst others. Although Skala Kallonis has fairly good tourism, it has not lost its fishing village atmosphere. The small village square is fairly quiet by day but comes alive in the evening with diners filling the tables which spill out into the road. If the resident pelican is still hungry, it usually wanders in and out of the tables around the tavernas begging for fish. Perhaps the most reliable time to see this highly domesticated pet is at the small fishing port in the morning as the fishing boats return.

Set out westwards from the town square and stay along the coast road on meeting the main road

Right: Sigri castle

Below: Windmill, Sigri

Right: Turkish minaret at Parakila

junction shortly. It feels more like a lake than a gulf as you drive along close to the waters edge here. Very shortly a sign announces Parakila. Immediately through the village, look carefully through the trees on the left to spot the minaret of a Turkish mosque. Park where a trail forks left and walk down the trail a hundred paces or so for a close view. Unfortunately, memories of the Turks are still too raw to consider this mosque and minaret as part of their history and heritage so it is being allowed to decay. Typically, as the Turks did with many of their sacred places and graveyards, they filled the grounds with flowers, this time tall blue iris, *Iris germanica*. It is a picture in springtime. From here the road leads to a higher level and very soon there are clear views of a large village, Agra, clinging high on the mountainside. It seems the most unlikely scenario from this point but, the road climbs the hillside to pass right through the centre of this village.

Beyond Agra barren terracotta mountains sweep and fold around green valleys all the way to Mesotopos and beyond, providing engaging and fascinating landscapes. Turn off left to drive down to Skala Eressou and park in the large car park just on entering this small village.

It is a small but beautiful resort with buckets of sand, at least enough for a small desert. Eressos is the birthplace of Sappho, the famous poetess from antiquity, but Eressos is not quite romantic enough so all the associations have been transferred to Skala Eressou. Expect to see her name cropping up all over the place.

Sappho (ca 612 - 580BC)

The great lyric poetess Sappho was born to an aristocratic family in Eressos around 612BC. Tradition tells that she, along with other aristocrats, was either banished or emigrated to Sicily around 596BC. It is said that she was married to Cercolas, a man from Andros.

She returned to Lesvos some time in her still young life and took a full part in society. It was custom for the women of good families to meet together informally to pass the time enjoying music and poetry. Sappho was a leading light at these meetings and attracted many admirers. Deeply immersed in arts and poetry, she went on to start a school for young ladies.

Her tender, harmonic poetry dwelt on the loves, jealousies and relationships of herself and her contemporaries. How her poems became known in her own lifetime is not really understood but what remained of her poems was published in the 3rd and 2nd centuries BC.

Ancient writers who had access to more of her work than exists today, claim that her poems show emotions stronger than mere friendship towards other women and allege that she was what we now term a lesbian. None of the existing works of Sappho show any hint of homosexuality so the truth may never actually be known.

Skala Eressou spreads itself out along the beach with plenty of bars and tavernas facing directly onto the beach and out to sea. The daytime atmosphere here extends to enjoying the beach and relaxing but the evenings are different with all the diners out along the front. It does not take too long to promenade here and take in the sights.

The best option for continuing on to Sigri is to go by the main road. There is a track which follows roughly the line of the coast between Eressos and Sigri but this is more suitable for a 4WD. Take the road back through Eressos itself to meet the Andissa Sigri main road. As you drive along from here, note the good surface road off left signposted to the petrified forest but save your visit until after Sigri. There is a very good museum at Sigri dedicated to the petrified forest which will fill in the background and make your eventual visit more interesting.

Just on entering Sigri, take the major road leading up left to the museum. For once, timing is not too critical since this museum opens all day (8am - 4.30pm, closed Monday longer in Summer). It is a modern museum with well presented displays and there are some fine examples of petrified trees in the grounds outside.

To explore Sigri, head back down the museum approach road, turn left and drive the short distance to the port area to park. Sigri is built on a headland with coastline on two sides of the town and is the most westerly settlement on the island. A fortress lies further out on the headland which was built by the Turks around 1757, strengthening the earlier Venetian fort built by Gattelusi.

Sigri is an isolated and very quiet resort appreciated by those who like to think they have found their own small island. Walking inland from the main harbour through the narrow streets leads over to a small sandy beach at the edge of town. There are tavernas around for catching up on refreshments and there is no finer place on the island to appreciate the sunset.

Head back out of Sigri to visit the petrified forest. With three trails to follow, there is a fair amount of walking involved up and down a hillside baked in sunshine. Fortunately, there is a snack bar just inside the entrance selling drinks.

The Petrified Forest

This unique natural monument has been recognised for its geological importance and protected as a European Geopark in 2000. This ensures its protection, management and development.

During a period of intense volcanic activity in the Aegean some twenty million years ago, volcanic lava poured over the western end of the island covering the existing forests to a huge depth. Tree trunks smothered by lava and starved of oxygen failed to burn but were preserved in the petrified state they are now seen. This preservation process retained many features of the tree, the character of the bark, the wood structure and the annual rings. Now, twenty million years on, they offer a window into the past. Experts have been able to identify these trees and gain a deep insight into the nature of the forests of that period.

Although the existence of the petrified forest has been known for many years, largely through erosion exposing some of the standing trunks, only in recent years has systematic work been undertaken and serious excavation started. There were plenty of surprises in store. The nature of the plant fossils and the type of trees found suggest that the climate on Lesvos was subtropical at that time.

Some of the massive trunks seen in various excavations are ancestors of the North American giant redwoods and the other significant discovery is a totally new species, *Pinoxylon paradoxum*, presumably a paradox because there is no known comparable species. It is believed to be a predecessor of today's pine trees and is classed in a new family, *Protopinaceae*, meaning literally 'the first pine'. There are modern representatives of trees in the petrified forest including poplars, laurels, maples, oaks and plane trees.

There are three trails around the park which are themed and all the petrified trunks included in the circuits are numbered. The first trail, the Blue Trail, is intended as a general introduction to the park and to petrified coniferous trees. The Green Trail, the longest, 1.3 miles (2.1km), leads through a section of the old forest with some massive trunks of ancient redwoods on view. There is a chance to see remnants of the paradox pine on the Red Trail, so look out for exhibits 50 - 55.

The collapsed volcanic crater seen on the return from Andissa

On leaving the petrified forest, return to the main road to head back towards Kalloni. Travelling between Eressos and Sigri, you may have noticed a church, Moni Ypsilou perched on the top of what may be a volcanic cone. Although there is not too much to see at the monastery, the view over the surrounding hillsides is good, especially towards sunset. The narrow access lies on the right and there is a one way system in operation up to the Moni. The monastery was founded originally in 800 and the monastery church built in 1101 but it was plundered several times by the Turks. Some restoration has recently taken place.

An interesting mountain drive lies ahead on the return to Kalloni. The route passes through a collapsed volcanic crater which starts around 3miles (5km) beyond Andissa. It is most easily recognised by the rocky gorge on the left hand side of the road. There is no proper viewing place or suitable place to stop but the gorge reaches about 0.75 miles (1.2km) in length. If time allows, visit Lesvos' only winery, the Methymneos Winery (open July-Sept) at Hidira, a 6km diversion from Vatausa. Turn right at Vatousa to Pterounda then right again through Revma.

At Skalahori keep on the main road towards Filia. Once you start descending towards Kalloni, good views open up over one of the island's most important monasteries, Moni Limonas, neatly laid out in rectangular formation with lots of satellite churches. The details of this monastery are included in Car Tour 2. There is an excellent old walking trail which leads from the monastery back down to Kalloni (see The Monk's Way). Continuing by car, Kalloni and the conclusion of the tour is soon reached.

Walk No 3: The Monk's Way

A beautiful old trail connects Moni Limonas first with Metochi, another monastery, and then Kalloni. This is a walk to enjoy and take at a leisurely pace so allow around two hours for the 3.75 miles (6km). It is exposed to the full heat of the sun all day long so be sure to carry some water and have sun protection, including a hat. The easiest way to organise transport is to taxi from Kalloni and walk back.

Goat gates referred to in the walk are usually temporary structures, either chicken wire stretched across the track or brushwood. They are intended to keep the goats from straying, not to keep people out so simply pass through and restore the gate to how it was found.

Start out from the front gate of the monastery and walk ahead with the monastery wall immediately on your right. Continue along with walls either side to pass under a concrete bridge. Keep ahead on a wide track where the road swings right into the monastery. At the end of a wire fence on the left, turn left into a track. There is an old wooden sign to Metochi which looks ready to fall off so it may or may not be still there. Continue along this track which wends its way through impoverished looking olive groves towards a long red-roofed rather grand goat house ahead. Pass through a goat gate very shortly to join a cobbled trail. As the trail swings right towards the grand goat house, stay ahead on a narrow but distinct cobbled trail, again with the faint possibility of the Metochi sign in place.

Very shortly the trail rises over the saddle and opens up sweeping views down to the Gulf of Kalloni and across to Mount Olympos. The trail along here is breathtaking in its construction, made of huge slabs of stone. The surrounding geology is equally fascinating and obviously the source of the slabs. Metochi soon comes into view and the trail ends just before a gate fastened with rope. Go through to the front of Metochi which is often used for seminars. It may be open but not to the general public.

Continue ahead along the route of the original trail by passing through the green gates ahead. Keep alongside the wall on the right but be prepared to dodge around natural springs, leaking hosepipes and boggy bits where necessary. Pass below a small chapel up left and continue ahead to meet another green gate which exits to a track. Turn left towards Kalloni and pass a white pumping station on the left. Ignore a track forking in from the right but turn right at the next junction, about 6 minutes from the gate. Cross a concrete bridge to reach a T junction. Turn left towards Kalloni and stay ahead on this road through the back of the town. Turn right at the next T junction to arrive at the main road right in the middle of Kalloni near the taxi rank.

CAR TOUR 2 :
THE MOUNTAINOUS NORTH

This car tour has a rich menu which includes Moni Limonas, one of Lesvos' largest and most important monasteries, two small adjacent resorts, Anaxos and Petra, the island's premier resort, the fortified town of Molyvos, a picture-postcard fishing port and spectacular mountain scenery. If you plan to lunch out, save it for Skala Sikaminias. Distances on this tour are not too great totalling around 60 miles (96km) but there are more than enough highlights to fill a day. The route described leads out of Kalloni through Dafia to Filia then cuts through to Skoutaros and along the north coast to Molyvos. After a short diversion from Molyvos to Eftalou, the onward route continues along the main road through Vafios to Sikaminias and down to Skala Sikaminias. The route back home takes you from Sikaminias towards Mandamados with a turn off leading through Kapi, Pelopi and Stipsi. This road is very narrow in places through the villages. From Stipsi you join the main Molyvos - Kalloni road.

Head out of Kalloni initially towards Molyvos but turn left very shortly into the Eressos and Sigri road. As you climb away from Kalloni, watch out for the slip road left leading down to Limonas Monastery, the first stop on this tour.

This extensive monastery was first

Above: Moni Limonas *Below:* Walking along the 'Monk's Way'

built in 1523 by the bishop of Mythimna, Ignatius Agalianus, on top of the ruins of an earlier Byzantine monastery. Ignatius later became a saint. The church itself is named in honour of the Archangel Michael (*Taxiarchis Mihail*). In the early years of the Turkish occupation it was the only intellectual centre on Lesvos and became guardian of the Greek language by running a secret Greek school. Over the years it collected together religious and artistic treasures, manuscripts, scrolls and parchments and now has a library of 2,500 volumes and more than 400 manuscripts dating from the 9th to the 19th century. It represents a priceless spiritual, intellectual and historical treasure. Some of these nationally important articles are on display in the museum.

The rustic cloisters are open to all but the church is strictly males only. Associated with the monastery is a female annex, Moni Mirsiniotissa also built by St Ignatius, which can be visited towards the end of this tour. Wandering around the cloisters is fascinating enough and the small cell once occupied by St Ignatius is open for inspection. There is a small zoo in the grounds and a snack bar for refreshments just outside the main entrance. October 13th and 14th, the Feast

Below left: Eftalou beach *Below right:* Fisherman, Skala Sikaminias harbour

of Agios Ignatius, are special days and are spent in celebration.

Continue on the tour by still heading towards Sigri but, on reaching Filia, look to turn right to cut across through Skoutaros to the north coast road. Hidden in the middle of Filia is an old Turkish mosque still with a minaret but it is obscured by the village houses and hard to see.

There are a couple of resorts to call in on the way which are worthy of a look but may not detain you too long, unless you want to swim. Anaxos is the first resort reached which is a relatively new family resort built around an excellent beach. Further along from Anaxos is Petra which nestles below a massive rock rising out of the plain like a flat-topped pinnacle. The church, Our Lady of the Sweet Kiss, on top of the rock is the focal point of this small village and all roads lead to it. It is not the only important church in town, Ag. Nikolaos, near a huge plane tree, contains important frescos and ancient icons. Also of interest here is the 18th century Vareltzidaina mansion, one of the early Turkish style buildings full of classical influence (open 8.30am - 7pm summer, - 3pm winter, closed Monday).

The next stop is Molyvos and be sure to park in the car park at the entrance to the town. Details of Molyvos are included in the Days Out section.

On leaving Molyvos, take the road from the car park leading to Eftalou. Once you have driven over the headland and back to sea level, watch out for the cobbled road off left just as the road reverts to track and starts to rise again. Park and walk down the road a short distance to the hot springs located within the white dome shaped building at the waters edge. There is a small charge to bathe in the hot springs but not to gain access to the beach beyond. Simply walk through the front and out of the side door. The beach is small, secluded and increasingly popular. In its quieter days, it was popular for nude bathing but less so now.

Hot Springs

With an endless history of fractured plates, volcanic activity, and earthquakes, geothermal activity on the island comes as no surprise. Unlike ancient times when powerful earthquakes destroyed cities, the island has not had an earthquake strong enough to cause serious damage since August 6th 1383. On this occasion the castle in Mytilene town was destroyed and many killed. There are still frequent shakes but all modern buildings are built to cope.

Hot springs occur at a number of places around the island. Although less valued for their curative properties in these days of modern medicine, there are still remarkable stories coming from users who find them extremely beneficial, especially for arthritis. The baths that have been commercialised include:

Eftalou: recently modernised and still operating, this spring has a water temperature of 43.6-46.5 degrees C and a radioactivity of 2.5 units. Bathing is beneficial for a variety of complaints including rheumatism, arthritis, sciatica, neuralgia, kidney and gall stones and gynaecological problems.

Polichnitos: the hottest springs in Europe with a water temperature of 76-91 degrees C and a radioactivity of 1.6 units. Suitable for rheumatism, arthritis, sciatica, gynaecological and dermatological problems.

Gulf of Gera: water temperature a rather pleasant 39.7 degrees C with a radioactivity of 1.8 units. Good for rheumatism, arthritis, kindney and gall stones, gynaecological complaints. Separate public baths for men and women.

Lisvori: lying not too far away from Polichnitos, Lisvori is another spring with a high water temperature at 69 degrees C and showing a radioactivity of 2.6 units. Recommended for rheumatism, arthritis, sciatica, neuralgia, kidney and gall stones and gynaecological problems.

Thermi: one of the oldest commercialised hot springs which also became the most important supported by an impressive hotel. Sadly the hotel is now closed but there is talk of a renovation programme. Thermi springs has a water temperature of 49.8 degrees C and a radioactivity of 0.8 units. It is beneficial for most of the complaints already listed but this time including digestive disorders and neurological ailments.,

Return to Molyvos to continue on this tour. Turn briefly towards Petra then take the left turn along the main road which leads through Vafios and Lepetimnos to Sikaminias. It is a steady climb into the mountains all the way to Sikaminias and then a sharp descent to the coast and Skala Sikaminias. Park at the earliest opportunity as you enter this small fishing village. All life centres around the picturesque fishing harbour given a picture post card quality by the small white church built on a rocky outcrop by the harbour mole. The church has a rather unusual name, Panagia tis Gorgonas, meaning the Virgin Mary Mermaid.

The harbour is surrounded by tavernas and Skala Sikaminias has become the top spot on the island for lunch, especially with the islanders themselves. If you prefer something shared by fewer people, there is a quieter option within walking distance, although you can also drive. Head eastward along the front at Skala Sikaminias and across the back of a small beach to find an old trail rising away from the coast. Follow this up to meet a track and turn left here to meet the road in about five minutes. Turn left at the road and head down to the beach at Kagia. Go right, behind the beach, to find a choice of two tavernas.

Leave Skala Sikaminias to climb back up to the main village, turn left towards Mandamados. After a

Petra beach

twisting ride around the hillside, the road off right to Kapi can easily be missed. The corniche road along the south side of Mount Lepetimnos gives excellent views at times down towards Ag. Paraskevi. Stipsi is reached soon enough where the road becomes much wider until it joins the main Molyvos - Kalloni road. Turn south to head back to Kalloni but, if you intend to visit Moni Mirsiniotissa, watch out for the right turn soon after descending the hillside and back on level road again approaching Kalloni.

CAR TOUR 3: THE DEEP SOUTH

A major highlight on this tour is the long, sandy beach at Vatera but there is plenty of exceptional and unusual scenery around the Gulf of Kalloni, including a view across the narrowest section, the remains of one of the important cities of antiquity and some towns and villages still set in old traditions. Make this a half day if you wish but taken at a leisurely pace, this 75 mile (120km) tour can easily stretch to a full day.

From Kalloni take the road out east towards Mytilene town. Look out for the flocks of flamingos on the salt pans as you cross the head of the gulf and take the road off right to Polichnitos. Should you wish to visit the Mesa Sanctuary (re-opens when a museum has been completed in 2005) carry on ahead on the Mytilene road for a short distance and look for the sign left to Mesa Sanctuary. The site contains the excavated ruins of a large temple to Aphrodite as well as an early Christian basilica.

Continue along the Polichnitos road which stays close to the gulf side for a time shortly passing a sheltered corner used as a harbour by a handful of fishing boats. From here the road sweeps inland briefly, returning to the coast at Achladeri recognised by a solitary taverna right on the water's edge. A great place for lunch or just for a cool beer. Park here to set off to find ancient Pyrrha.

Ancient Pyrrha is one of the very earliest settlements on Lesvos dating back as far as the 9th century BC. It grew into a powerful city state controlling the territory all down this eastern side of the gulf. The acropolis part of the city was built on a small offshore island but the settlement spread onto the adjacent mainland. A massive earthquake in the year 231BC destroyed not just the city but also the island which now lies below the sea. There are still blocks of stone and other remnants of this city to be seen along a short walk. Cross in front of the taverna and just keep going along the coast for several hundred yards and simply look around for all the distinct and recognisable remains of ancient Pyrrha.

From Achladeri the road meets cross roads where the main road goes to the left and the track right is the eventual return route. Follow the main road initially through a straight avenue of cypress trees before it starts to climb into low hills. At the T junction turn right to progress through Vasilika towards Polichnitos. Polichnitos itself is a traditional, bustling agricultural town which could not be further removed from present day tourism. Many of the old imposing mansions and neo-classical buildings tell of its wealth and importance in the past. Like much of eastern Lesvos, olives are a major product in the whole of this area.

Below: Fishermen on the Gulf of Kalloni

The Olive

Known from Crete as early as 3,500BC, the olive has been central to the existence of the Mediterranean peoples for millennia. Although grown primarily for oil for cooking, the oil is also used as a lubricant, for lighting, soap making and in ointments and liniments for the skin. The fruit itself, the olive, is also eaten

During the early Turkish occupation, wheat and wine were the chief products of Lesvos. At some time in the 18th century, a social transformation took place. The Greeks managed to take back ownership of a large part of the land from the Turks creating a powerful class of landowners. Olive oil became the new growth industry, restrained in the early days only by the restriction on trade imposed under Turkish occupation. Once free of the yoke, the farming of olives and the production of olive oil became a huge business on Lesvos. The island now has an incredible 11 million olive trees which cover around 80% of the arable land or 28% of the total land area. With a population of around 88,000 it works out at 125 olive trees per head. Virtually everybody on the island owns an olive grove or two which will have been in the family for generations. Normally, on the death of the parents, the assets, including olive groves, are divided between the children. It is not unusual to see paint blobs on olive trees indicating a demarkation of a grove.

The tree is evergreen with leathery lance-shaped leaves which are dark green above and silvery beneath. With age the trunks become gnarled and twisted adding considerably to the character of the tree. It takes 4-8 years for a tree to start bearing fruit but full production is not reached until after 15-20 years and it may then continue for centuries with proper care. The tree is erratic in that not every year produces a good crop, unless a suitable regime of irrigation and feeding is rigorously followed, but more often dry farming is employed and good crops are expected every other year. Whitish flowers borne in loose clusters arrive in late spring which rely on the wind for pollination. The fruit which follows takes 6-8 months to reach full maturity for only then does it give the maximum yield of oil. This means that harvesting takes place throughout the winter months, from December through until March, the perfect complement to working in the tourist season. Fruits for eating are collected before maturity and need special treatment with dilute caustic lye and salt to kill the extreme bitterness. There are hundreds of named varieties of olives, both for oil and for eating, which are propagated from hard wood cuttings or from leaf cuttings under mist propagation.

Picking olives is hard work and is still very manual. Often the only aid available is a long stick to beat the branches to encourage the fruit to fall. Nets below the tree collect the olives and the leaves which fall with the fruit. A sieve of narrow slots which allows only the leaves to fall through is used to clean the product, another manual process, before the bags of olives are taken to the factory to be pressed. 100kg of fresh olives yields about 20 -30kg of oil.

Olive oil is produced in a selection of grades, the very finest oil from the first pressing is known as virgin oil and this is the grade preferred for salad dressing. It is a good buy to take home too and can be found on supermarket shelves in 1 or 5 litre containers.

The wood too is of great value. It is very hard, strongly grained and takes a fine polish, ideal for carving, cabinet work and toys. It is good too as a slow burning fuel and for making charcoal for which the Greeks have a great demand.

Botanically, the olive, *Olea europea,* belongs to the Oleaceae family and has some interesting and familiar relatives including ash, privet, jasmine and lilac.

Watch out in the centre of Polichnitos for a sharp left turn at the first cross roads and another left turn almost immediately for Vatera. Shortly down this road there is a sign leading off left to the thermal spa. The main road by-passes Vrissa but there are access roads north and south of the town. Park by the southern access road, by the Eko petrol station, and walk in. Vrissa is worth a stop to see what Greece without tourism used to be like. Old men sit outside tavernas idly talking, their coffee cups or ouzo glasses rarely moving but content in their observation of life. The women critically turning often tired looking vegetables outside the mini markets wondering whether to purchase. A passing pickup truck might turn heads for a moment then everybody settles back into their relaxed timeless existence. Apart from the ambience there is a small but excellent Natural History Museum (open 9.30am - 3pm; closed Monday & Tuesday) on the left when entering the village.

Vatera greets you on arrival at the coast road. The resort, like the beach, ribbons, either side of this junction, there is no real heart or old centre. Turn right first to start a local exploration, heading out to Cape Fokas to see the ancient temple of Dionysos. Turn inland at the end of the beach where the road continues as track and turn left over the bridge (there is a short river walk to try which starts from this point).

Walk No. 4:
The Terrapin Trail

This circular walk is an easy, level stroll of just 2.25 miles (3.6km) which takes less than one hour. It follows up along one side of the river, crosses a higher bridge and returns down the other. Route finding is very easy so few instructions are required.

Those staying in Vatera will need to walk out westwards and continue inland where the road ends and continues as track. The bridge is reached very shortly, cross the bridge and turn right to walk with the river on your right. There is an instant countryside ambience as you walk past olive groves. This reedy river is good for birds but they are more often heard than seen. Go quietly where there is a view of the waters edge and look for striped-neck terrapins. There are hundreds along this river bank but they tend to dive underwater when disturbed.

Carry on along the riverside to reach the next concrete bridge, cross over and turn left again to walk back to the starting point, still alongside the river.

which is very popular with the locals. Return to Vatera by the same route to explore the huge stretch of beach. Spring is a wonderful time to see the beach in glorious colour. The flowers at the rear of the beach give a mass display second to none and the variety of species is surprising too with some real specialities like *Trigonella coerulescence* which looks rather like a large, deep blue clover and a deep red poppy with large, intense black markings, *Papaver argemone ssp nigrotinctum*.

Turn left again over the bridge and follow this track as it leads finally onto the headland. The fenced ruins of the temple of Dionysos lie over on the right. Not a big site but a fantastic location with a church, Ag. Fokas, which shares its name with the headland. There is a seasonal taverna too

Name That Church

The countryside sometimes seems littered with small, mostly white churches. No matter how simple, each one has a name which can be worked out from the icons contained within. It is fun to try and challenging even with these guidelines. Knowing the Greek alphabet helps for identifying the saints but when ancient script is used, it can be even more difficult.

If the doorway in the iconstasis is central, then the icon of the Virgin Mary should be on the left and the icon of the saint after which the church is named to the left of the Virgin Mary. Christ is on the right of the doorway and St John the Baptist to the right of Christ.

If the doorway is not central, it is usually on the left taking up the space normally reserved for the icon dedicated to the saint of the church. Now, the icon of the saint to which the church is dedicated is then placed on the right of Christ.

It works most of the time but there are still pitfalls to watch out for, especially when the church is dedicated to two or more saints.

Above: Polichnitos   *Opposite page:* Kato Stavros

As you progress along the beach, facilities run out and the road turns inland towards Stavros. This is a pleasant drive though leafy countryside but it is wise to turn at Stavros and not be tempted further. A track leads through the mountains from Kato Stavros to Ambeliko which is well stabilised and driveable (soon to be surfaced).

Return from here through Vatera to Polichnitos. Turn right at the first cross-roads and keep straight ahead, with care, at the second signposted Skala Polichnitou. Watch out after about 2miles (3km) for the left turn to Nifida. The tiny fishing settlement of Nifida ribbons along a narrow beach but it does offer accommodation and tavernas in season. The fascination here is seeing across the mouth of the gulf and realising how narrow it really is at this point. Return by the same route back to the Skala Polichnitou road and on to Skala Polichnitou. This is another small resort which is principally the fishing village of Polichnitos and where the locals come to eat fish, especially on a Sunday. It has a good relaxed atmosphere and makes an ideal lunch stop.

The onward route from here is along stabilised tracks right the way to Achladeri. After seriously heavy rains, it is advisable to cut out this section and return to Kalloni via Polichnitos, otherwise it is a great route back. Follow the road out of Skala Polichnitou towards the salt pans, arriving immediately at a roundabout, take the second exit, a track, from the roundabout to pass behind the salt pans. There are still more flamingos to see here, sometimes in really large numbers. Stay with the track initially following signs to Skamnioudi which brings you to the surfaced road leading between Lisvori and Skamnioudi. Turn left if you wish to visit the small fishing harbour and taverna at Skamnioudi otherwise continue across now following signs to Achladeri. Still on track, keep going to the Vasilika - Skala Vasilikon road and turn down left. It is easy to navigate now as you follow the road down into Skala Vasilikon, another quiet place with tavernas. From here follow the track along the coast, again enjoying views from the very edge of the sea. The church by the shore, reached very shortly, is Ag. Pavlos. This is the spot where St Paul is believed to have landed when he came to preach the gospel to the Lesvians. Very shortly, the track swings inland to connect with the Achladeri road used in the outward journey. Turn left at this junction and follow, now on familiar territory, all the way back to Kalloni.

CAR TOUR 4: THE HEIGHTS OF OLYMPOS

This tour explores the heights surrounding Mount Olympos in the eastern side of the island. Mount Olympos is a distinctive limestone mountain which can be seen for miles around, even from Kalloni. Highlights of this tour include Agiassos, Plomari, Ag. Isidoros, the Gulf of Gera and, perhaps above all, spectacular and varied scenery. Although the tour is not too long at 80 miles (128km), much of the driving over the

Ta Mylelia (little mill)

In a quiet pastoral setting, not far from Ipios, lies a 250 year old restored water mill which has been set back to work and grinds 150-200kg of flour daily. The flour is sent off to Athens where it is used to make a whole range of sun-dried pastas which are available in the Mylelia shop. There are lots of other products there too and most have some connection with Lesvos. This is the place to buy olive oil with herb's, walnuts, fresh rosemary, marinated black olives and a host of other tempting natural products.

Apart from the commercial activities, it is an open-air museum with an old donkey powered olive press, a 300 year old open-air church next to the modern church and the old mill itself. The sylvan ambience and the isolation gives this a real period context.

Visitors are welcome, if only to look around. It lies off the Agiassos - Mytilene road. Coming from the Mytilene direction, look for a narrow track off right about 0.5mile (1km) after the Ipios turn off. Follow this narrow track until the bridge is crossed (0.4km) and park in the wide area. Enter through a small garden gate and wander through to the old mill.

mountains will be slow so it is wise to allow a full day. The route takes you first to Agiassos then right over the top of the mountains and down to Plomari on the south coast. A long winding section of this road over the mountains is stabilsed track. Anyone anxious about driving on this sort of track in the mountains should consider this tour inappropriate. From Plomari the main road is followed along the Gulf of Gera then back to base on the Mytilene - Kalloni road.

Leave Kalloni on the Mytilene road but take the right turn to Achladeri when you have crossed the head of the Gulf of Kalloni. This is an alternative route to Agiassos to save covering too much of the same territory on the return leg. Continue around the gulf enjoying extensive views until the road leads you left inland into the hills. Turn left at the T junction and, a little further along, look out for the Big Lake, Megali Limni, which is not a lake as such now just an extensive cultivated flat area. Turn right at the Agiassos junction and watch out very shortly for the road off left signposted to Sanatorio. This road by-passes Agiassos which has already been detailed in the 'Days Out' section. If you wish to visit the town carry on straight ahead but return to this junction to continue.

Views of Mount Olympos are impressive from the Sanatorio road which winds through the top of Agiassos. Be sure to make the sharp left turn on entering the top of the town. The open road greets you within minutes and views down right over Agiassos reveal its

Above left: Plomari   *Above right:* Ag. Isidoros beach

surprisingly large size. Pine woods and cherry orchards line the road on the way to the Sanatorio beyond where chestnut woods take over. This surfaced road leads in a steady climb without a hint that it eventually becomes a stabilised track at the summit. The vistas around here offer unrivalled mountainous scenery in an area as isolated as any in Europe. A winding descent leads along ridges and through valleys eventually to habitation, Megalochori. From here a surfaced road leads all the way down to the coast and Plomari.

A one-way system in Plomari filters traffic towards the coast and the fishing port. Between fishing, olive oil, tanneries and ouzo factories, Plomari is a hive of industry. It is about a century now since it was at the peak of its activities and there are some very fine buildings around from that period. Most tourists visiting this region prefer to stay at Ag. Isidoros, just a short distance to the east. On the right, just before reaching Ag. Isiodoros, is the Barbayanni ouzo factory which many believe makes the best ouzo on the island. It is open for visitors Monday to Friday during working hours. On offer here is a museum, a brief look at the manufacturing facility and a tasting of the different qualities of ouzo.

Ag. Isidoros is another of the smaller resorts which attracts most visitors in high season. It has a good beach and plenty of supporting facilities.

The onward route swings around to head north towards the Gulf of Gera. Look for the Perama sign off right on reaching Skopelos and cut across the plain to join the coast at Perama. It is only a small village but there is a passenger ferry from here across the gulf to Koundouroudia. The ferry crosses virtually on demand and the crossing takes only a few minutes. On the other side are small tavernas right on the water's edge which are a great place to have an ouzo or a fish lunch.

Continue north along the edge of the gulf until the main road is rejoined. Tanneries along the gulf side were responsible for polluting this gulf but since their demise the pollution has steadily diminished.

Turn left on joining the Mytilene - Kalloni road and drive back through the pine forests to Kalloni.

Below: Kremasti bridge near Agia Paraskevi. Take the road through Agia Paraskevi toward Napi and look for the wide track off left signposted Kremasti

Ouzo

Wine has a by-product in the form of grape skins, seeds, pulp and stems which can be distilled to produce a strong spirit, known collectively as raki or souma. Powerful flavours can be introduced by the infusion of certain herb's, like fennel or aniseed, before distillation. Ouzo has grown out of this process. No longer is it made from the wine residues but from pure alcohol, made either from molasses or raisins, distilled with aniseed and other botanicals. Well made ouzo contains around 46% alcohol and is usually taken with ice or water. Dilution with water liberates the aromatic oil anethole, introduced from the aniseed, which turns the drink milky, sometimes more so or less so depending on the actual manufacture. Generally, dense cloudiness indicates high quality. To the casual drinker, all ouzos taste much the same but the various brand names have different followings, some achieving wider recognition throughout the country than others. Plomari ouzo is rated one of the best.

For the Greeks, ouzo is more than just a drink, it is blue sky, warm air, sunshine and even more, it is the breath of the soul, a drink to share for male bonding. Traditionally, it must be taken with a little food, nuts or mezedes. Mezedes is a small plate of food, typically a few small bite size pieces of bread, some olives, a bit of cheese, a meat ball or anything that the taverna is cooking that day. Now it is usually a few nuts but in some of the older villages ouzo is still served with mezedes.

Ouzo tasting and factory tours are available at "Barbayanni" in Plomari and "Mini" ouzo distillery in Mytilene.

CAR TOUR 5:
THE SOUTH EAST CORNER

There is a whole peninsula south of Mytilene town which is good to drive but little explored. The coast north of Mytilene has some places of interest so these are conveniently included in this tour. Lying in wait on this tour are water's edge tavernas at Koundouroudia, a picturesque cove at Ermogenis, ancient and modern Thermi with its tower houses and a Roman aqueduct at Moria. There is around 75 miles (120km) of driving in store but plenty of opportunity to stop off.

Set off from Kalloni on the Mytilene road and keep heading towards the capital until you reach the head of the second gulf, the Gulf of Gera. As you pass around the gulf, and just where the main road cuts inland on a sharp bend, look for the road off right signposted to Kendro and Pirgi. Once on this road stay ahead through the olive groves and expect a stretch of unsurfaced road part way along. Turn right on meeting the Loutra road and just keep going, ignoring signs off to Loutra and Skala Loutron, until the end of the surfaced road is reached. Park here wherever you can find space but be aware this is where the bus turns around too. It is easy to move on thinking there is nothing to see but walk down to the sea edge and the ferry landing stage. There are tavernas either side, both sharing an idyllic view across the gulf. Ta Asteria, the taverna to the left on the boatyard side, is open all year and also controls the small ferry. It is a great spot to relax over lunch and watch the small ferry ploughing backward and forward. It is very inexpensive to cross so if you have not had the opportunity to visit Perama on the far side, now is your chance.

Track back to the Loutra junction and turn right to travel through Loutra. Take the road south, signposted Ag. Ermogenis, to head down the peninsula. Look out shortly for the diversion off right to visit Ag. Ermogenis. This picturesque cove with a small, sandy beach is the nearest playground for the people of Mytilene town so it tends to be busy at weekends. Return to the main road to continue south around the peninsula. Views of the open sea and the near land mass of Asia Minor serve to remind just how close this island lies to Turkey. As you travel around the southern tip and start to head north, the route takes you past the airport and into Mytilene town.

Things to see and do in Mytilene town are described in the Days Out section. If you plan to spend time there now, try and park in the large car park on the right before the harbour. There is another chance to park later if this part is too busy.

Drive through Mytilene by staying with the sea front road all around the harbour until almost to the ferry port, turn inland with the main flow of traffic to pass close to the castle. The second chance to park is now, as you emerge in the north harbour. Locate the north end of Ermou Street which emerges in this harbour to walk back into the main shopping area.

Keep driving northwards along the east coast and ignore the bypass for the moment. For a flavour of Panagiouda and Pamfila, stay with the coastal road and leave the by-pass until the return. Neither are large places and both have a small harbour. Keep going northwards

Ancient stone showing Malteses Cross reused in a modern building, typical at Thermi

until the road leads back to the coast at Thermi, or more correctly Pyrgi Thermi, and park further along near the fishing port. Looking at the map there seems to be a confusion of Pyrgi and Thermi but, in reality, it is three parts of the same settlement. *Pyrgi* means 'tower' in Greek and the village of Pyrgi Thermi is characterised by its tower houses. Thermi came into usage as a name after the Romans built a thermal baths next to the hot springs and effectively converted it into a holiday resort. The word *paralia* translates into seashore or beach so Paralia Pyrgi is no more than the descriptive name for the development around the port. There is still one more part, the very old village, built inland away from the sea called Loutropoli Thermis, the 'bath city of Thermi'.

Kounduroudia

Ag. Ermogenis

Tower Houses of Pyrgi

At the end of the 19th century, there were as many as 160 three storey, stone built *pyrgoi* or tower houses in Pyrgi. Originally built in the period when pirates were still active, they were fortified by necessity in this location so close to the sea. The vertical configuration of the house, the square floor plan, the lack of windows or openings in the lower storeys, the iron grills on the first floor windows and the overhanging balconies were all important defensive features. Exterior doors were of a heavy construction often with a hole above or a hole beneath the first floor which allowed scalding liquids to be thrown down on aggressors.

Interior defences included sealing off the stair well with a heavy trap door which could be firmly secured with bolts or bars, and most houses would have a secret hiding place somewhere where endangered residents could hide themselves away as a last resort.

These tower houses became the fashion towards the end of the 18th century and were often the second homes of the rich bourgeoisie probably from Mytilene. It is where families would spend the summer or oversee the olive picking in winter.

Thermi is a very ancient settlement, occupied from prehistoric times and probably continuously since. Although there have been no major excavations, small, isolated digs suggest there was a large Roman settlement which spread over from the port to the church of Ag. Nikolaos. Since this became an important spa resort, it was very likely that there was a Roman port and there are foundations of a large Roman building just under the sea.

Artemis, the goddess and protector of thermal springs was most certainly worshipped here but excavations have as yet failed to reveal a temple. The only evidence that has turned up is from inscribed stones, marble reliefs and column fragments which have been recycled and used in the walls of many of the older buildings in the region.

The whole area is a haven for archaeologists or for anyone

prepared to look with keen eyes at the existing buildings and within some of the smaller old churches for ancient stones. This is a place for wandering around, finding the bath house behind the crumbling hotel and walking up the hill to the old town.

In the hills not far from Thermi is the Monastery of Ag. Rafael with its two storied church. Rafael is credited with working miracles and, complete with accommodation and tavernas, is a place of pilgrimage for Greeks from far and wide.

To continue the tour, head back down south and take the bypass road to miss Pamfila but turn right along the new Moria road. This emerges on the old road between Moria and the Gulf of Gera so turn left here to head back into Moria along a one way system. As you drive through the village, watch carefully in the centre for the aqueduct sign pointing right, down a narrow street. Drive past here and park where the road widens a little further along. Walk back and down the narrow street for a few minutes to find the towering aqueduct. It was built by the Romans to carry water from Mount Olympos to Mytilene town, a distance of over 16 miles (26km).

From Moria, keep driving through and turn sharp left beyond the church to go back following the one way system in the opposite direction. This road leads down to the Gulf of Gera where a right turn sets you back towards Kalloni.

The Forgotten Saints: Rafael, Nicholas and Irene

April 9th 1463 AD, after the fall of Constantinople, was just another day at the monastery at Kyres, near Thermi, where Rafael was the Abbot and Nicholas a Deacon. Visiting that day was 12 year-old Irene, daughter of the mayor of Thermi, with her father and the village teacher. Disaster struck, the Turks raided the monastery and the three saints were cruelly tortured. Rafael's torture ended when his head was sawn off, Nicholas died of heart failure under torture and the young Irene was tortured in front of her father and burnt alive in a clay cask. All three were matyred for the sake of their Christian faith.

These saints remained unknown for almost 500 years, throughout the Turkish occupation and beyond until 1959. Suddenly the saints made their presence known, appearing in visions and dreams to the people of Lesvos. They guided believers to their own graves and brought about many miraculous cures. They are very special saints to the people of Lesvos and all three are deeply revered. Pilgrims from all over the world visit Lesvos to attend the Monastery of Rafael.

Their memory is celebrated on the first Tuesday after Easter Sunday.

Roman aqueduct at Moria

Theophilos the Painter

Born in Varia in 1873, Theophilos was a man who loved to paint. He painted murals in houses, churches and even in tavernas. He would often paint for free but other times it was in exchange for food or maybe a glass of ouzo. Teriad, a wealthy art critic and publisher, met Theophilos in 1928 and was immediately impressed by the primitive quality and force of his work. He persuaded Theophilos to paint on canvas so that his work could be appreciated by future generations. Theophilos blossomed under the challenge of painting on canvas and produced some 120 paintings which many regard as his finest.

Reproductions of the painter's work can be seen all over the island and bought as postcards. Teriad continued his support by building a museum to house some of his most famous paintings. Next to the museum is the Teriad Library which houses 29 of Teriad's books.

The museum is in Varia. Take the airport road south out of Mytilene, look for the right turn to Varia and continue to a T junction. Turn left here and soon turn left on a corner signposted to the museum.

GETTING THERE:

The easiest is by charter flight from the UK but this option is only available between May and October. For those wishing to get to the island the rest of the year, the only practical solution is to fly via Athens with BA; Olympic Airways or Easyjet.

There are regular flights from Athens out to Lesvos, both by Olympic (online reservations: www.olympicairways.co.uk; e-mail:sales@ olympicairways.co.uk; tel.sales 0870 606 0460) and Aegean Airways (online reservations: www.aegeanair.com) these can be booked through travel agents in the UK, Thomas Cook for example, in conjunction with an international flight between the UK and Athens. It does not matter if the international flight is a charter or schedule and usually it is possible to complete the journey in one day.

There are advantages to travelling the whole journey with Olympic Airlines in that your luggage is transferred onward to the island without the need to collect it at Athens and check in again. Olympic Airways runs schedule flights from both Heathrow and Manchester Airport. With other airlines it may not always be possible to transfer luggage but these days all flights land at Athens International Airport so there is no longer any need to change airports.

Regional flights within the UK connect BA/BA and BMI/Olympic Airlines. If all connecting flights are on the same ticket, passengers are covered along the route for delays which may result in a missed flight.

ACCOMMODATION

Outside July and August, there is plenty of accommodation available around the island and travellers on a flight only basis should have a good choice. High season is a different matter. The Greeks themselves flood to the island together with many other Europeans. In this period, especially August, it is important to book in advance.

Hotels:

There is a wide selection of hotels on the island spread throughout all the major resorts. Unfortunately, there is no central booking agency on the island but there is a useful web site at www.filoxenia.net which gives a fair list of hotels with details and contact numbers. Otherwise enquiries should be made through the Greek National Tourist Office in London Greece (www.gnto.co.uk)

Fact File

Rooms and Apartments:

There are plenty of rooms and apartments to let but no overall letting agency. Sites to check out are: www.the-vatera-specialist.com which offers rooms and hotels in Vatera and across the island and www.malemi-com

CAR HIRE

Car hire is popular and many visitors take a car for three or four days which is generally enough to see the various parts of the island. A current driving licence is required for EU nationals and others should have an International Driving Permit. The hirer must be over 21, some companies insist on 23, for a car and 25 for a jeep or a minibus.

Cars can easily be hired on Lesvos but sometimes a better deal can be arranged by booking and paying in advance of departure, not necessarily through a tour company but through companies like Transhire (Tel 0870 789 8000) or Holiday Autos (www.holidayautos.co.uk) Tel 0870 400 4447 which offer good rates and include full insurance and unlimited mileage. These companies operate through an agent on the island and usually offer rates significantly lower than those available from the agent on the spot.

When hiring from an agency on the island, check the advertised rates. These are very often the basic rates exclusive of insurance, mileage and tax. Third party insurance is compulsory under Greek law and this cost will be added to the hire charge. An additional optional insurance is collision damage waiver (CDW) and it is imperative to take it. This cannot be stressed too strongly. Should you be unfortunate enough to be involved in an accident without CDW insurance and the costs cannot be recovered from a third party then the consequences can be frightening. At best you may be faced with a huge repair bill, at worst you could end up in jail until it is fully paid. On short one or two day hires mileage is often limited to 100km/day and a rate applies for excess kilometres. On top of all this is VAT at 18%.

Tyres and damage to the underside of the car are mostly excluded from the insurance cover and insurance may not be valid on unmade roads. Take time when you are accepting the car to inspect the tyres and, if not fully satisfied, don't accept the vehicle. It is worth a moment too to check that lights and indicators are fully operational. Greek law demands that a car must also carry a fire extinguisher, first aid kit and a warning triangle.

Motorcycles

Above comments on insurance apply also to hiring a motorcycle or moped. Insist on a crash helmet since the law says very clearly that these must be worn. Most agencies have helmets now but only produce them if they think they are about to lose business. Make sure before you depart that the lights and indicators work

See also Driving on Lesvos

CHANGING MONEY

Banks are in short supply outside Mytilene town and Kalloni but there are plenty of ATM's around and some exchange cash machines. Check that the ATM displays a full range of symbols including Cirrus and Maestro then use your normal bank card and pin number as you would at home. It is the easiest and cheapest way of obtaining cash.

For those travelling into Mytilene or Kalloni intending to use banks, the opening hours are as follows: Mon. - Thurs. 8.00am - 2.00pm, Friday 8.00am - 1.30pm. Post Offices sometimes offer exchange facilities and are open weekdays from 7.30am - 2.00pm, closed on Saturday and Sunday.

CHILDREN'S ADULTS ENTERTAINMENT

Wildlife park: there is a small wildlife park in Agia Paraskevi set up and run by the Wildlife Hospital which relies on public donations to keep it going. The park is used as a convalescence centre and permanent home for patients unfit to be released back into the wild. Here ia a chance to see, at close quarters, a variety of owls and birds of prey, also tortoises, hedgehogs and waterfowl. Telephone 2253 032 006 to fix a visiting time.

To find the park, head into Agia Paraskevi and go right with the main road. Turn right again, almost immediately, between a church and the school to reach the Park.

Donkey rides: there is a donkey farm near Molyvos which offers donkey rides and donkey treks. Find it off the Eftalou road.

CONSULATES

There are no consuls on the island but the Tourist Police are empowered to issue a temporary exit in the event of a lost or stolen passport. If there is sufficient time, they will fax the Embassy in Athens to obtain a temporary passport.

Nearest foreign Embassies and Consulates are:

Australia
37 D Soutsou Street & Tsocha
115 21 Athens
Tel 210 645 0404

Canada
4 I. Genadiou Street
115 21 Athens
Tel 210 927 3400

USA
Embassy-Consulate
91 Vass. Sophias Avenue
101 60 Athens
Tel 210 721 2951

UK
1 Ploutarchou Street
106 75 Athens
Tel 210 727 2600

Fact File

CRIME AND THEFT

On an island like Lesvos, crime and theft levels are low and incidences of violence rare. There is no need to feel threatened in any way, even throughout the evening, but it is sensible to be cautious late at night, especially women on their own.

Many hotels have safety deposit boxes available for guests at a small charge. Otherwise, keep valuables out of sight. This is particularly true if you have a car. Cameras, personal stereos and the like are best carried with you but if you need to leave them in the car make sure they are locked in the boot.

If you are unfortunate enough to suffer a loss through theft or carelessness then report it to the Tourist Police. There is a form to complete if an insurance claim is contemplated.

If your loss includes a passport then you will need to contact the Tourist Police (see Consulates).

CURRENCY & CREDIT CARDS

Greece was amongst the first twelve countries to replace their own national currency with the euro. Notes of legal tender have values of 500, 200, 100, 50, 20, 10 and 5 euros. One and two euro coins are available along with 50, 20, 10, 5, 2 and 1 cent coins (cents are called 'lepta' in Greece) . The notes are identical in design in all countries of the eurozone but the coins have a national design on one side.

Travellers cheques and hard currencies are freely accepted at banks and post offices. Credit cards and charge cards are widely accepted in hotels but not all shops or smaller restaurants and tavernas.

Always take your passport when changing money. Even though the production of a passport may not be a necessary requirement, the Greeks rely on them as a means of identification. You may even be asked for it when purchasing an internal flight ticket. The cost of changing money in terms of commission does vary and it pays to check; normally the cheapest place is at a bank and the worst place is the hotel reception.

See Changing Money

DRIVING ON LESVOS

Driving on Lesvos is on the right hand side of the road and over-taking on the left. In the event of an accident where the driver was proven to be on the wrong side of the road, the insurance is invalidated. Unless there are signs indicating otherwise, the speed limits are as follows: built-up areas 50kph (31mph), outside built-up areas 90kph (56mph). Radar speed checks are in regular use so it pays to observe the limits carefully. Seat belts must be worn by law. The use of main beam headlights in towns and cities is forbidden as is the carrying of petrol in cans.

A driver must always carry a passport, driving licence and the car hire documents or incur a fine if stopped. There are regular and frequent police checks on the island.

Unleaded petrol (amolivthi venzini) is freely available on Lesvos. The grades of petrol (venzini) normally on offer are unleaded, Super-unleaded and Super at 96/98 octane. Diesel is also widely available and, like petrol, is sold by the litre.

Parking in Mytilene town is a problem but there is a large car park near the sea front just south of the centre. For detailed advice on parking see Mytilene in the Out & About section. It pays to observe street parking restrictions, often ignored by the Greeks but illegal parking can result in a ticket and a hefty fine, especially for visitors. The ticket indicates the amount of the fine and where and when to pay it. The police are not empowered to collect on the spot fines.

With one of the worst accident rates in Europe, driving in Greece demands a cautious attitude from the onset. The discipline shown by the majority of drivers in western European countries, which brings order to traffic flow, is often missing from Greek drivers but drivers on Lesvos are, in the main, a little more orderly. Drive with your own safety in mind. Another major hazard is the state of the roads. Pot holes are always a danger and can be encountered unexpectedly even on well surfaced roads. A line of rocks on the road guiding you towards the centre is the usual warning of edge subsidence and there will often be no other warning signs. Minor roads, which are well surfaced, may suddenly become unmetalled. Road works may have no hazard warning signs or irregular ones such as a pile of earth or a milk crate with a small flag.

Here is a quick check on some of the hazards frequently encountered: uncertain rights of way, limited road markings, narrow roads, sharp edges, potholes, ill placed road signs, Greek drivers driving the wrong way through a one way system, sheep, goats and donkeys, motorcyclists without lights, and pedestrians where there are no footpaths.

Accidents and Legal Advice

In the event of an accident involving personal injury or damage to property, both the law and your insurance require that it is reported to the police (Tel 100).

Breakdowns

It is a legal requirement to place a warning triangle 100m/yds behind the car. Next step is to contact the car hire agency.

Disabled Facilities

Whilst there is an awareness of this problem, few practical steps have been taken to improve matters. Mytilene town is a crowded and difficult place for wheel chairs and very few towns outside have pavements. Where pavements exist they are often full of trees making passage difficult. Ramps up and down pavements are few and far between. On a more positive note, resorts like Skala Kallonis, Vatera, Anaxos, Petra and Thermi are fairly level, and a number of the hotels have ground floor access where is would be possible to gain access to standard rooms. Unfortunately, widened doorways and bathrooms for disabled are a thing of the future.

ELECTRICITY

Mains electricity is supplied at 220 volts AC. Electrical equipment should be fitted with a continental two pin plug or an appropriate adapter used. A wide selection of adapters for local plugs to interchange between two and three pin (not UK three pin) are available cheaply on the island.

EMERGENCY TELEPHONE NUMBERS

Police 100

Fire 199

Tourist Police171

Ambulance 166

GREEK TIME

Greek normal time is 2 hours ahead of GMT. The clocks advance one hour for summertime starting the last Sunday in March and ending the last Sunday in October in line with Europe.

HEALTH CARE

For minor ailments like headaches, mosquito bites or tummy upsets, head for the chemist shop (farmakion). If you need a further supply of prescription drugs be sure to take a copy of your prescription and the chances are that you will be able to get them, and cheaply too. Pharmacies are open normal shop hours and most seem to speak English. Certain chemist shops are on a rota to provide a 24 hour service and information for the nearest is posted in the pharmacy window.

If it is a doctor or dentist you require, the chemist shop should again be able to assist.

Problems really start if hospital treatment is required. European countries have reciprocal arrangements with the Greeks for free medical treatment, subject to certain restrictions. For this reason British visitors should take an E111 form obtained from the Post Office. The story does not end there. To operate the scheme you need to find the local Greek Social Insurance office (IKA) who, after inspecting your E111, will direct you to a registered doctor or dentist. If you are in a region remote from the IKA office in Mytilene or Kalloni then you must pay privately for your treatment and present your bills to an IKA official before you leave the island. Up to half your costs may be refunded. The best answer is to ensure that you have adequate holiday insurance cover, although the insurer may still expect to offset some cost by use of the E111 form.

Emergency treatment, sunburn, broken bones etc., is free in state hospitals. The situation is less happy if you require treatment as an in patient. In many of these hospitals, nursing care is restricted only to medical treatment and it is left to the family to supply general nursing care, drinks, food and even blankets.

It is generally preferable to activate private medical insurance.

Health hazards

Stomach upsets are perhaps the most common ailment. The excessive olive oil used in cooking and over salads can be a cause of queasy stomachs so take care with oily foods, at least to start with. The digestive system adjusts to this within a few days and you can soon eat giant beans swimming in oil without fear. Squeeze plenty of fresh lemon over your food to counter the oil and, if still troubled, an acidic drink, like Coca-Cola, helps to settle things. Drinking wine to excess can cause similar symptoms too. More serious are the upsets caused by bad food or contaminated water. Generally it is better to drink bottled water which is freely available and cheap in the shops and supermarkets. Avoiding food poisoning is not always possible in any society but there are elementary precautions that can help. Many tavernas prepare cooked meat dishes for the lunch time trade and these are left keeping warm until finally sold. If they are still there in the evening, and they often are, avoid them. Ask for something which will require grilling or roasting.

Care is needed on the beach to avoid stings from jelly fish and, in rocky regions, from sea urchins. If you are unlucky enough to have a brush with the latter it is important to ensure that all the spines are properly removed. Wearing beach shoes will give your feet some protection from stings of this nature.

See also Mosquitoes

HOLIDAY INSURANCE

Whichever holiday insurance you choose, make sure that the cover for medical expenses is more than adequate. It helps too if there is an emergency 24 hour contact to take care of arrangements, including repatriation if necessary. Injuries caused whilst taking part in certain hazardous pursuits are normally excluded from medical cover. Look carefully at the specified hazardous pursuits; in recent times, injuries caused by riding a moped or motorbike have been added to the list by some insurers.

INTERNATIONAL DIALLING CODES

Codes from Greece are as follows: UK & Northern Ireland 0044: United States & Canada 001: Australia 0061: New Zealand: 0064. See also Telephone Services.

LOST PROPERTY

This should be reported immediately to the Tourist Police, tel 171. It is particularly important if an insurance claim is to be made.

MAPS

The publisher Road Editions is producing excellent maps for many parts of Greece based on the Hellenic Army maps. These are the most accurate maps available to the general public and there is one for Lesvos (No. 212; 1:70,000) which can be bought on the island or in advance, at a higher price, from Stamfords in London or the Map Shop in Upton upon Severn.

Generally, road signposting is fairly good on the island with Greek signs displayed first and the Latinised version a little nearer the junction.

MOSQUITOES

Mosquitoes feed most actively at dusk and dawn but they can still be a nuisance throughout the evening and night. If you sit or dine outside in the evening, particularly near trees, either cover up your arms and legs or use insect repellent. For the hotel room, an electric machine which slowly vaporises a pellet is very effective, especially with the windows closed, and there are sprays available for more instant results if intruders are spotted. Anthisan anti histamine cream is an effective calming treatment for bites, particularly if applied immediately. If you collect a bite while dining in a taverna, try either lemon juice or vinegar, both are effective treatments.

MUSEUMS

There is a charge for admission except in some State or Municipal museums where entrance is often free on a Sunday during winter. Monday is now the general closing day.

The museums are closed too, or open only for a short while, on certain public holiday. See Public Holidays & Festivals.

NATIONAL TOURIST OFFICES

Leaflets on Lesvos, and general information on Greece is available before departure from the
Greek National Tourist Office, addresses as follows:

UK and Ireland
4 Conduit Street,
London W1R 0DJ
tel 020 7734 599

USA
645 Fifth Avenue,
Olympic Tower (5th Floor),
New York NY10022
tel 421 57777;
168 North Michigan Avenue,
Chicago, Illinois 60601
tel 782 1084
611 West 6th Street,
Suite 2198 Los Angeles,
California 90017
tel 6266 696

Australia & New Zealand
51-57 Pitt Street, Sydney,
NSW 2000
tel 9241 1663

On Lesvos the Greek National
Tourist Office is located by the
ferry port terminal in Mytilene,
tel: 2251 042511

NEWSPAPERS & MAGAZINES

Most British newspapers and a selection from European countries are usually available in virtually all centres of tourism in the main summer season. They are available in Mytilene town all year around from the kiosk on the promenade, near Hotel Lesvian. Mostly they are one day late although some are available the same day. Expect a fair mark up in price. The place to look for newspapers is in tourist shops, supermarkets and at kiosks (periptera).
A selection of English and European magazines is also available.

NIGHT LIFE

Lesvos is not exactly renowned for its night life and some discos are only open at weekends. Things are more lively in the main season where night life can be found in the bars, nightclubs, discos and restaurants which organise Greek dancing.

NUDISM

Topless bathing is commonplace on all public beaches on Lesvos. Nude bathing is not acceptable but is practised with discretion on some of the more remote and secluded beaches.

PASSPORTS AND JABS

There are no visa requirements for EU citizens or other English speaking nationals (USA, Australia, Canada, New Zealand) for visits of up to 3 months. All that is required is a valid passport.

Certain inoculations are advisable for all travellers (hepatitis A & B, tetanus, typhoid and T B.) but none are mandatory for Greece.

PETS

Cats and dogs require health and rabies inoculation certificates issued by a veterinary authority in the country of origin not more than 12 months (cats 6 months) and not less than 6 days prior to arrival.

PHARMACIES

Pharmacies open Monday & Wednesday 8am - 1.30pm. Tues., Thurs., & Fri. 8am - 1.30pm & 5.30- 8.30pm and Saturday 8am - 1.30pm.. There is also a duty rosta for Pharmacies so that at least one in the vicinity is open on Saturday and Sunday. Usually a note on the door of the pharmacy details the duty chemist.

PHOTOGRAPHY

Signs which show a picture of a camera crossed out indicate a prohibited area for photography. Notices of this kind are posted near every military establishment, no matter how small or insignificant. Disregard this at your peril. The Greeks are still paranoiac about security and anyone found using a camera in a prohibited zone faces unpleasant consequences. The photographer may be held in custody whilst the film is developed and inspected and at worst detained overnight. Remember that Lesvos, with its close proximity to Turkey, is a militarised island so special vigilance is required not to disobey any signs.

Photography with a camera mounted on a tripod is prohibited in museums as is the use of flash in some. Video cameras are often subject to a fee.

POSTAL SERVICES

Post Offices open on weekdays from 7.30am - 2pm. They are closed on Saturday and Sunday.

Stamps (grammatosima) can be purchased at the post office, sometimes at a special counter, or at a kiosk (periptero). They are also available in many shops and some of the larger hotels but usually at a slightly increased price. An express service for urgent letters is available.

PUBLIC HOLIDAYS AND FESTIVALS

The Greek calendar overflows with red letter days; public holidays, Saints days and festivals. On public holidays, banks, shops and offices are closed although restaurants and tavernas normally stay open. Public transport is often interrupted too, reverting either to a Sunday service or to none at all. Many petrol stations also close during public holidays. The days to watch out for are;

1 January – New Year's Day
6 January – Epiphany
25 March – Greek Independence Day;
Monday before Lent – Clean Monday
April – Good Friday & Easter Monday
1 May – May Day
Whit Monday
15 August – Assumption of the Blessed Virgin Mary
28 October – 'Ochi' Day
25 December – Christmas Day
26 December – Boxing Day

Easter is variable and does not always coincide with Easter throughout the rest of Europe.

Name-days are one reason why the calendar is so full of celebrations. It has been a long tradition for Greeks to ignore birthdays and celebrate instead the special day of their saint, of which there are many. If you see people wandering around with cake boxes neatly tied with fancy ribbon, or bunches of flowers or unusual activity around one of the many churches, then the chances are that it is a name day. The custom is for the person celebrating to offer hospitality to friends, to neighbours and to almost anyone who will partake of a little ouzo and refreshments.

Some of the big name days to watch out for are:

23 April – St. George's day; all Georges everywhere celebrate their special day but in addition it is also the national day of Greece. If April 23rd falls within holy week, the week immediately before Easter, then celebrations are delayed until Easter Monday.

21 May – Saints Konstantinos and Eleni.

29 June – St. Peter and St Paul

9 August – Irene

15 August – Assumption of the Blessed Virgin Mary. This is the day when millions of Marias celebrate and an important day in the religious calendar often marked by local pilgrimages or festivals.

8 November – for all Michaels and Gabriels.

6 December – the feast of St. Nicholas.

Fact File

Easter is the biggest and most important celebration of the year. The arrival of Carnival time starts the long build up. This festival takes place throughout the three weeks before Lent and may commence as early as late January. Fancy dress is an important part of the tradition throughout the whole of Greece. It arises from the period of Turkish occupation when the Greeks were banned from conducting these celebrations. Driven under cover, festivities continued with people disguised to prevent recognition. Now it is firmly rooted into the custom and fancy dress and costumes are worn at all events. The children wander the streets in fancy dress and traditionally show defiance by wearing their disguises on the last school day of Carnival.

All this comes to an abrupt end with a complete change of mood on 'Clean Monday' (Kathari Deutera), the Monday before Lent. This is a public holiday when families traditionally exodus to the country to fly kites and to picnic, which mostly means heading to a taverna. Special meat-free menus are the order of the day.

It is back to the quiet life throughout Lent which is still strictly observed by many, especially in country regions. Serious preparations for Easter start on Maundy Thursday. How hens are persuaded to lay so actively for the occasion remains a mystery but shoppers are out buying eggs, not by the tens but by the hundreds. The rest of the day is spent in boiling the eggs and dying them red in the process. The colour red is supposed to have protective powers and the first egg dyed belongs to the Virgin.

Good Friday is a day of complete fast and widely observed. In tourist regions tavernas are open and life goes on as normal but in country areas it can be difficult or even impossible to find food. Yellow or brown 'impure' candles are on sale everywhere ready for the evening church service. The sombre mood of the day is heightened by the continual tolling of church bells. It is a day for remembering their own dead; graves are visited and wreaths are laid. In the evening, the burial of Christ is the most moving and widely attended service in the whole of the Greek Orthodox calendar. The *epitafios*, the funeral bier of Christ, is centre stage in the services which start around 9 o'clock in the evening. Garlanded with fresh flowers and with a gilded canopy, the *epitafios* bearing the coffin of Christ is ceremoniously taken from church in dignified candlelit procession followed by silent mourners and accompanied by bands playing solemn music. The processions from all the local churches meet in the town square for a further short service. This is the most poignant moment of the evening, cafes close, tavernas close and there is not one Greek who would willingly miss it. The processions return slowly to their churches, stopping at each street corner for a short prayer.

Saturday brings an air of expectancy. For the evening service, yellow candles are replaced with white. Funereal drapes are removed in the churches and decorations of laurel and myrtle take their place. In dimly lit churches everywhere, services begin.

Slowly the light intensity increases reaching full brightness at midnight when priests triumphantly chant 'Christ is risen' (*Christos anesti*). The sanctuary doors open to show that the *epitafios* is empty. Light from the priest's candle is passed to the congregation and that flame is rapidly passed from candle to candle until it reaches the waiting crowds outside. Fire crackers drown the clamour of the church bells as the crowd erupts in joyous celebration and greetings of '*Christos anesti*' ring out loudest of all. The crowds disperse shortly carefully protecting their burning candle; it is a good omen to enter the home with the flame still burning and make a sooty sign of the cross on the door lintel. The moment they are back home, the Easter feasting starts.

Sunday is a day of out and out rejoicing. The big occasion of the day is roasting the lamb or goat. Charcoal fires are lit early in the morning and the spit roasting is done with loving care over some 5 hours with copious quantities of ouzo or retsina to help things along. All those red eggs now appear and are used in friendly competition. Each contestant taps their egg hard enough to break an opponent's but not their own.

Easter Monday has no special ceremonies or rituals and passes as any normal public holiday.

Above left and right: Religious festival, Panagiri

Fact File

CULTURAL EVENTS

Religious fairs, *panagiria*, are commonplace in the summer months. *Panagiria* are a celebration of the name day of a particular church or monastery and usually held in the vicinity of the establishment. Celebrations are colourful, often beginning on the eve of the name day and continue throughout the actual day. Eating, drinking and dancing are central to any celebration for the Greeks so the barbecue is certain to be in operation. When the crowds are big enough, vendors join in selling just about anything, baubles, bangles and beads.

A word of warning too. Each town and village has its own saint's day and sometimes, depending on the local whim and the phase of the moon, a holiday is called. This decision is often not taken until the day before so there is no way you can plan for such eventualities.

PUBLIC TOILETS

The most usual sign is WC with figures to indicate ladies (gynaikon) and gents (andron). Cafes provide the best hope of toilets even though it may be necessary to purchase a drink.

Mytilene has some modern toilets next to the theatre, on the seaward side of the taxi rank.

PUBLIC TRANSPORT

Buses

The long distance bus service on Lesvos is not especially good. Green and cream buses from country districts head into Mytilene in the mornings and head back to the village when the shops close after lunch. Saturday has a reduced service and there are no buses on Sunday except perhaps for July and August. Printed timetables are usually hard to obtain.

A local service of blue buses serving Mytilene town and environs operates from the same bus station on the sea front just south of the town

Taxis

Taxis are freely available in Mytilene and most tourist resorts.

Greek taxis drivers are not the most honest in the world and it pays either to check the price before the journey, if it is for a lengthy ride, or better still, insist that the meter be used. This displays the cumulative fare in euros. The rate of charges and surcharges are all fixed. Legitimate small surcharges are allowed for a sizeable piece of luggage, for attending an airport or port for the benefit of passengers, and for late night or very early morning travel. Surcharges are permitted too at holiday times, especially Christmas and Easter. Picking up a second fare is allowed too so you may find yourself sharing a taxi, but not the fare.

Fact File

SHOPPING

Regulations on opening hours have changed recently to adjust to market needs. Different regions have their own views on this so there is now greater confusion than ever over opening times. Big supermarkets and department stores open: Monday - Friday 8am - 8.pm. Saturday 8am - 3pm. Other shops open Monday & Wednesday 8am - 1.30pm. Tues., Thurs., & Fri. 8am - 1.30pm & 5.30 - 8.30pm and Saturday 8am - 1.30pm.

In tourist areas, shopping hours are much more relaxed. Tourist shops and supermarkets in particular are open all day long but butchers, bakers and the like tend to observe more restricted hours.

SPORTS & PASTIMES

Walking: Lesvos offers excellent walking opportunities for all grades of walkers. The mountains around Agiassos are particularly beautiful and there are old donkeys trails in various parts of the island which offer walks with an ancient ambience. The best walking book for the island is 'Landscapes of Lesvos' published by Sunflower Books (www.sunflowerbooks.co.uk) and written by Brian & Eileen Anderson.

Wind surfing: available at most of the main resorts

Water-skiing & Parascending: limited availabilty at some of the larger resorts.

Scuba diving: Strictly prohibited unless in the control of a recognised diving school and only in designated areas. With so many antiquities in the waters around Greece, it is forbidden to remove anything from the sea bed and infringements normally result in a prison sentence.

SUNBATHING

Sunburn and sunstroke can easily spoil your holiday and considerable care needs to be exercised, especially in the early days. The sun is very burning even on a hazy day so do not be deceived and continue to use sun protection. Crawling beneath a parasol isn't necessarily the full answer since the sun's rays reflect to some extent from the sand. Avoid, if possible, sunbathing in the middle of the day when the sun is at its highest and most direct. Sun creams help considerably but, at least for the first few days, take some very light clothing to cover up and control the exposure of your skin to the sun. A slowly acquired tan lasts longer.

Even mild sunburn can be painful and may cause a chill feeling but if fever, vomiting or blistering occur then professional help is essential.

Fact File

Above left and right: Souvenirs

Right: Windsurfing, Anaxos beach

TELEPHONE SERVICES

Hotels usually offer a telephone service, often from the room, but expect to pay a premium for the convenience.

Telephone booths on the island take phone cards and these are both convenient and economical. Cards are available from shops or kiosks, especially those nearest the telephone, and the cost per unit is exactly the same as the OTE (Telecommunications Office) charge.

International dialling codes from Greece are as follows: UK & Northern Ireland 0044: United States & Canada 001: Australia 0061: New Zealand: 0064.

SWIMMING

There is good swimming off many beaches on the island but there is not always a system of warning flags to indicate unsafe conditions., although the main beaches do have lifeguards on duty. It is absolutely essential to use common sense when the sea is rough or strong currents are flowing and avoid taking unnecessary risks.

TIPPING

There are no hard and fast rules on tipping, especially since bills by law already include a 17% service charge. Normally, the Greeks simply leave behind the small change after a meal and perhaps the best guide is to reward only for good service in a restaurant. Taxi drivers expect a tip as does the chamber maid in the hotel otherwise it is entirely by discretion.

WATER

Sources of drinking water vary on the island but it is safe for cleaning teeth. It is advisable to drink only bottled water which is freely available.

Index

VISITORS GUIDES

CITIES	ISLANDS	REGIONS
Oxford	**Northern Cyprus**	**Ticino**
ISBN 1 84306 022 1	ISBN 1 84306 056 6	ISBN 1 901522 97 0
Pages 96	Pages 176	Pages 208
£6.50	£9.95	£8.95
Includes places to visit on the outskirts of Oxford	The authors live and work in Cyprus and they drew on their extensive local knowledge to produce this comprehensive guide	Ticino is an extension of the Italian Lakes. This guide covers the area around Lake Lagarno and Lake Maggiore
Bruges	Gran Canaria	Cornwall & The Isles of Scilly
Cracow	Isle of Wight	Dordogne
Hereford	Kefalonia	Languedoc
Riga and its beaches	Mull, Iona & Staffa	Vendee
	Tenerife	
	Zakinthos	

visit **www.landmarkpublishing.co.uk** for a full listing

Published in the UK by
Landmark Publishing Ltd,
Ashbourne Hall, Cokayne Avenue, Ashbourne, Derbyshire DE6 1EJ England
Tel: (01335) 347349 Fax: (01335) 347303
e-mail: sales@landmarkpublishing.co.uk
website: landmarkpublishing.co.uk

ISBN 1 84306 118 X

Print: Gutenberg Press Ltd, Malta
Design & Cartography: Mark Titterton

Front cover: The white church of Virgin Mary Mermaid, Skala Sikaminias
Back cover, top: Kremasti bridge near Agia Paraskevi
Back cover, bottom: Ag. Isidoros beach

All photographs supplied by the authors

DISCLAIMER
While every care has been taken to ensure that the information in this book
is as accurate as possible at the time of publication, the publishers
and author accept no responsibility for any loss, injury or
inconvenience sustained by anyone using this book.